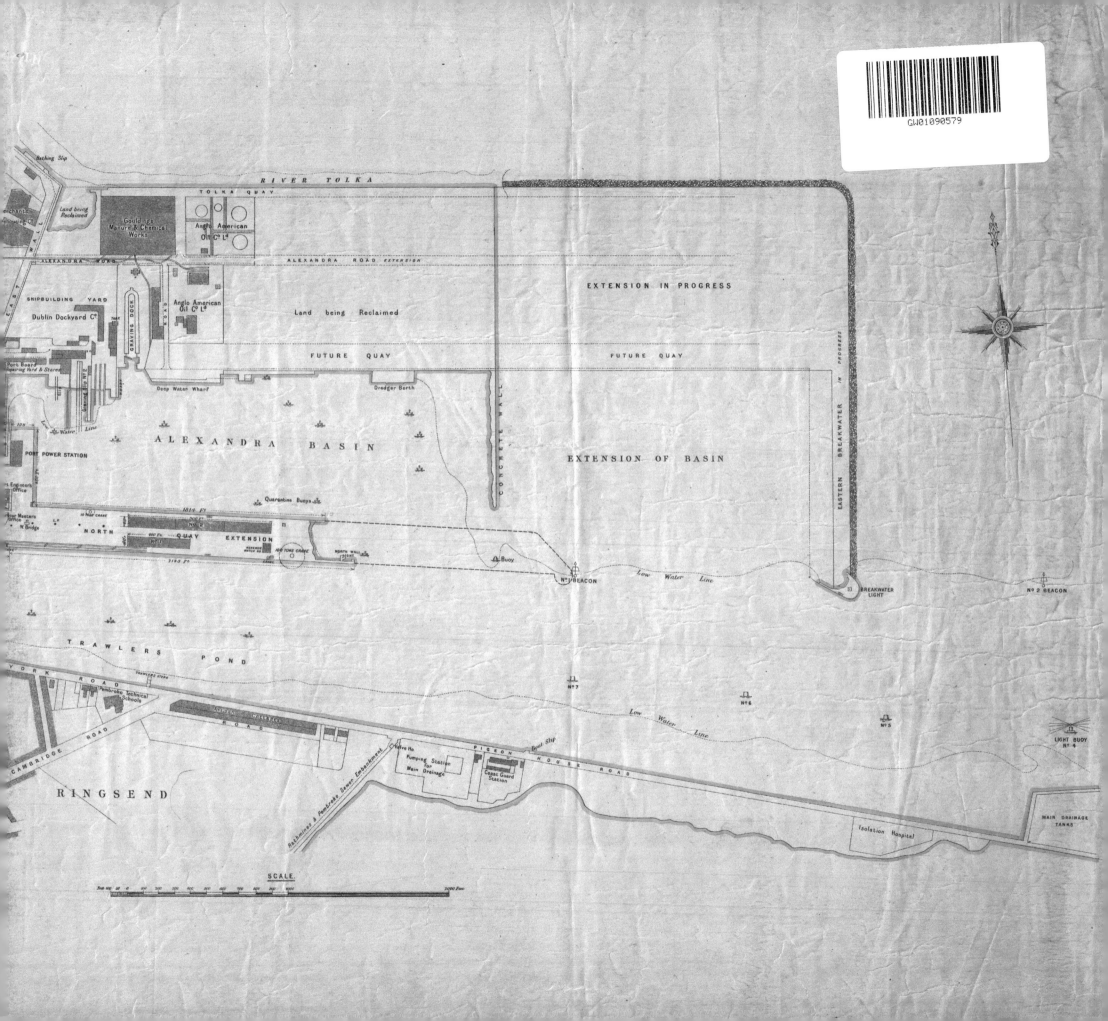

Bindon Blood Stoney
1828–1909

John Purser Griffith
1848–1938

Dublin Port Chief Engineers

Ronald Cox

Published by the Dublin Port Company in association with Engineers Ireland
©2023 Dublin Port Company and Engineers Ireland.

Book design by Boyle Design Group.

Foreword

IN THE EARLY 20th century the concept of town planning as a profession began to emerge and the Civics Institute of Ireland held an international competition to create a plan for Dublin which was won by Professor Abercrombie of University of Liverpool. Due to the violent conflict that impacted Dublin, with a Rising in 1916 followed by a War of Independence and Civil War the report *Dublin of the Future* - the New Town Plan was not published until 1922. In the foreword of the report two famous Dublin Port Engineers are mentioned. John Purser Griffith's description of "Dublin from its geographical position and lines of communication is the natural gateway to the greater part of Ireland and should be treated as a National and not merely a local asset" is quoted. To reinforce their argument against the then current piecemeal planning and squalor the authors quote a poem by Bindon Blood Stoney:

> *Then prove we now with best endeavour.*
> *What from our efforts yet may spring:*
> *He justly is despised who never*
> *Did thoughts to aid his labours bring.*

The fact that these two Grand Old Men of Irish Engineering and Port employees are quoted in the foreword shows the professional admiration for both men which Ronald Cox covers so eloquently in this book. Bindon Blood Stoney was Dublin Port Engineer from 1862 to 1899 and the modern city of Dublin along the River Liffey reflects his engineering prowess in the bridges and quay walls he built using his wonderful Diving Bell. When John Purser Griffith took over he would champion the city and the port and from 1899 to 1909 he helped modernise Dublin Port, reconstructing the North and South quays, electrifying the cranes with the port's own power station and reorganising dredging operations with a new modern suction dredger, The Sandpiper.

It is to Dr Cox's credit that he has taken his detailed research over many years on these two engineers and has created this wonderful book containing previously unseen photographs from the Dublin Port Archive to tell their story.

Lar Joye
Port Heritage Director
January 2023

Preface

IN 1990, the author was commissioned by the then Dublin Port & Docks Board to compile a biographical sketch of one of the most illustrious of the civil engineers to be associated with the port over its long history, *Bindon Blood Stoney*. The research, writing and publication phases of the initial project were supported by the Board and a biographical monograph published for the Institution of Engineers of Ireland (now Engineers Ireland) by Irish Engineering Publications Ltd. [ISBN 0 904083 02 0].

The author later presented a paper in 1998 to a joint meeting of the Institution of Engineers of Ireland Civil Division and Heritage Society on *John Purser Griffith*, who served as Stoney's assistant for twenty-seven years, before becoming his successor as Chief Port Engineer. The paper was published by the Centre for Civil Engineering Heritage at the Trinity College School of Engineering for the Institution of Engineers of Ireland. [ISBN 0 9522597 2 9]

The projects would not have been possible without the considerable assistance of the late Gerald Daly (1928-1998), then Honorary Archivist to the Dublin Port & Docks Board. Access to the letters and other archival material in the Board's possession was made much easier due to Gerry's tireless efforts and no query went unanswered for long.

This book consists of lightly edited versions of the two previous publications and is published by the Dublin Port Company, with the permission of Engineers Ireland, in support of the heritage activities of the company. The references for the 1990 publication were in the form of a bibliography of sources consulted, whereas the references for the 1998 paper generally followed the Chicago format of referencing.

The author of the text is an Engineering Historian and a Visiting Research Fellow in the Department of Civil, Structural & Environmental Engineering at Trinity College Dublin. He is a Member of the Institution of Civil Engineers, a Fellow of the Institution of Engineers of Ireland, a Fellow of the Irish Academy of Engineering, and a Member of the American Society of Civil Engineers. Recent books include Ireland's Bridges (2003), Engineering Ireland (2006), Ireland's Civil Engineering Heritage (2013), Called to Serve (2013) and Called to Serve Two (2019). The author acknowledges with thanks the contribution of Marta Lopez and Lar Joye in the sourcing of many of the illustrations from the Dublin Port Archives.

Contents

T H E R E A D E R of Harry Gilligan's excellent treatise on the History of Dublin Port *(Published by Gill & Macmillan in 1988)* will quickly realise that the development of the Harbour and Port of Dublin was in the hands of a number of inspiring and colourful characters.

The second half of the nineteenth century and the early years of the following century witnessed a great expansion in world trade and demands by shipping companies for secure deep-water berthage in the major ports could no longer be ignored.

As Chief Port Engineer, Bindon Blood Stoney bridged the period during which the Corporation for Improving and Preserving the Port of Dublin *(commonly known as the Ballast Board)* was replaced in 1867 by the Dublin Port & Docks Board, thus paving the way for the acceleration of engineering work leading to the creation of a modern deep-water port to serve an expanding economy. He was heavily involved in directing all the engineering work in the port, including the rebuilding of two of the major bridges spanning the river Liffey.

John Purser Griffith served as assistant engineer to Bindon Blood Stoney at Dublin Port, before taking over as Engineer-in-Chief in 1898. During his time at the port, Purser Griffith was responsible for the introduction of an extensive system of dredging and land reclamation, and the electrification of the port. During the course of a long career in the port and as an independent consulting engineer, he made a major contribution to the engineering profession and to the development of the Irish nation.

Bindon Blood Stoney

1828–1909

Stoney's early life, education and academic career

Family roots

The earliest records extant show that the Stoneys hailed from Kettlewell near Skipton in West Yorkshire, the name probably deriving from the stony tracts in those parts. There was, however, a tradition that the name Stoney came from the anglicised version of Mulclohy, the name of an Irish Sept descended from Maolclochach ('cloch'-Irish, a stone), 101st in traced descent from Adam through the royal line of Milesius (1800 BC)

Whatever about the early beginnings of the family, the marriage of Bindon Blood Stoney's 17th century forefather, George Stoney of Kettlewell, to one Mary Moorhouse of Rilston (near Kettlewell in Wharfedale) is recorded in the Rilston Parish Church register for the 6th January, 1675 (OS).

Towards the end of the 17th century, following the death of his mother, George Stoney appears to have mortgaged his small Yorkshire estate for the sum of £800 and emigrated to Ireland. He took advantage of William Ill's inducements to English Protestants with capital to settle there. George and Mary settled around 1692 at Knockshegowna in North Tipperary to the east of Borrisokane and near the border with King's County (now county Offaly).

Two of George's sons, Thomas and James, also moved with the family to Ireland and, of these, the eldest son Thomas interests us the most. In 1712, Thomas married Sarah Robinson of Knockshegowna, the Robinsons having migrated from county Durham, and went to live at Greyfort, a house leased from the Saunders family, near Borrisokane.

Thomas Stoney's eldest son, George, was born at Greyfort in 1713. It would appear from his diaries and letters that he was eminently possessed of common sense and energy and, it was said, the shrewdness of Yorkshire and the dash of Tipperary!

Acting on what he considered to be the sound economic principle that 'a man's income should increase with his family', George added year by year to his patrimony, and was able to give handsome fortunes to his six daughters and left four of his sons sufficient landed property to start them off in life as gentlemen (The remaining son had a scandalous affair with a lady of noble birth and was disinherited, but that's another story!). George of Greyfort died in 1787 and was interred in the spacious vault that he had provided for himself and others of his family in the churchyard at Borrisokane. (Greyfort later passed from the family and degenerated into a farm house).

To his third son in particular, James Johnston, George left lands in county Offaly, including Oakley Park (originally Ballymoney) near Parsonstown (now called Birr). The story goes that James Johnston Stoney, when only a boy, was sent by his father to Ballymoney to check up on the steward who was suspected of dishonesty. At the time, the old castle was used as a dwelling, but was supposed to be haunted by the ghost of some mediaeval chieftain. In the middle of the night James was awakened by the clanking of someone in armour coming up the lighted winding stairs to the bedroom. Nothing daunted, he lighted a lamp, seized a pistol, and confronted the 'ghost', who fled to the steward's room, closely pursued by James, who there discovered that it was none other than the steward himself, encased in a sheet and encircled with plough chains. James's father was so pleased with his son's brave conduct that he promised to leave him Ballymoney (later renamed Oakley Park) and this he did.

James Johnston Stoney died in 1824 and the property later passed from the family. Other branches of the family acquired through marriage, Portland Park and Emell Castle in North Tipperary. In fact, North Tipperary and Offaly became home to many members of the Stoney family and marrying into local families was quite commonplace. An indication of the concentrations of the Stoneys in these counties may be had from an examination of the entrance records of the University of Dublin (Trinity College), which show that, between 1790 and 1850, 28 male Stoneys entered the College, of whom no fewer than 20 were from either Tipperary or Offaly. No doubt that, if Trinity had admitted women during the period in question, many more Stoneys would have been afforded the opportunity of furthering their education at Trinity!

James Johnston Stoney had married Catherine Baker of Lismacue, their eldest son George in turn marrying Anne, the daughter of Bindon Blood of Cranagher near Ennis in county Clare. George and Anne's first born was George Johnstone (born 15.2.1826, died 5.7.1911), who preceded to a distinguished scientific career and who was for 25 years Secretary to the Queens University in Ireland. He made original contributions to the study of physical optics, of molecular physics, of the kinetic theory of gases and introduced the word 'electron' into scientific vocabulary.

Their second son Bindon Blood Stoney was born at Oakley Park on the 13th June, 1828.

Right:
Rilston Church

Far right:
East End and Interior view of Borrisokane Church showing the Stoney Vault and Stoney Pew and Tablet to the memory of George Robert Stoney of Greyfort

Childhood education

Stoney's childhood was spent on the family estate in county Offaly at a time of relative prosperity. He had the benefit of a private education. As he progressed towards manhood, time was running out for many in Ireland as the successive famines forced more and more of her people to board the emigrant ships for a better life in America and elsewhere.

The Stoney's country property in Ireland had been of considerable value during the early years of the nineteenth century. Those were times of large profits for agricultural undertakings, the Napoleonic Wars conferring an artificial value on home produce. Irish property fell in value when the wars ceased, and country gentlemen found that encumbrances incurred during the more prosperous times, including the results of lavish hospitality, were not so easily met as in the good times. Poverty fell upon them and the terrible times of the Irish Famine (1846-48), intensified by the policy of the day, which decreed the local raising of the Poor Law rate just where the famine was most severe, completed the ruin of many Irish families in those districts where the unfortunate tenants stood most in need of the landlord's assistance.

Bindon's father had died a few years earlier and the family property had to be sold; it fetched about eight years' purchase of the reduced rental, and the Stoneys' widowed mother and her children had no other means. As was the case with many country families who had lost their landed property, the Stoney's moved to Dublin and the children turned to professional careers in order to make their way in the world. It was a strenuous time in this younger society in Dublin, and one of much mutual helpfulness. In fact, Bindon and his brother were forced to earn the expense of their University fees by giving grinds, a not unknown feature of College life, even in today's more prosperous world.

The Stoney's country property in Ireland had been of considerable value during the early years of the nineteenth century. Those were times of large profits for agricultural undertakings, the Napoleonic Wars conferring an artificial value on home produce.

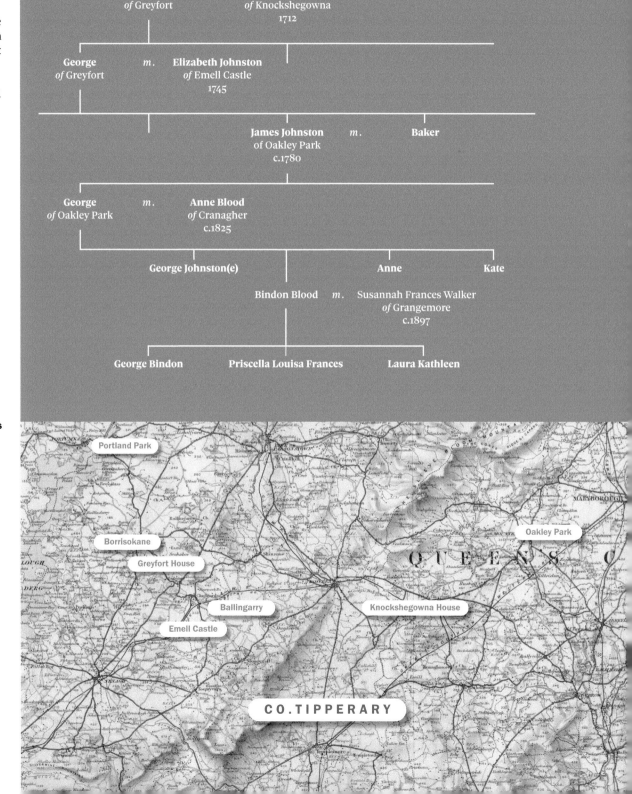

PART *of* STONEY FAMILY TREE

George Stoney *of* Kettlewell 6th Jan. m. **Mary Moorhouse** *of* Rilston 1675 (OS)

Thomas *of* Greyfort m. **Sarah Robinson** *of* Knockshegowna 1712

George *of* Greyfort m. **Elizabeth Johnston** *of* Emell Castle 1745

James Johnston of Oakley Park c.1780 m. **Baker**

George *of* Oakley Park m. **Anne Blood** *of* Cranagher c.1825

George Johnston(e)   **Anne**   **Kate**

Bindon Blood m. **Susannah Frances Walker** *of* Grangemore c.1897

George Bindon   **Priscella Louisa Frances**   **Laura Kathleen**

Stoney family associations with North Tipperary and Offaly. (Ordanance Survey of Ireland 1862)

Portland Park

Borrisokane

Greyfort House

Oakley Park

QUEEN'S C

MARYBOROUGH

Ballingarry

Knockshegowna House

Emell Castle

CO. TIPPERARY

Academic career

Having successfully Matriculated in Latin and Greek, Bindon entered Trinity College Dublin on July 1st, 1845, at the age of 17, as a Pensioner, the word originally meaning one who paid a fixed sum annually and not, as now, the recipient of such. Pensioners ranked above the Sizars, who were allowed free education in return for the performance of certain, at one time menial, duties, and below the Fellow Commoners, who paid double fees and enjoyed several privileges, including that of being able to complete the College course in three years instead of four. Pensioners were normally the sons of persons of moderate means, as in Bindon's case. At the time of Bindon's entry to Trinity College, the Queen's Colleges in Cork, Galway and Belfast had just launched courses in engineering, some three years after the School of Engineering in Trinity was founded. The entrance records of the College confirm that Bindon's father was 'Generosus defunctus', or 'Gentleman, deceased'. George Longfield, a Junior Fellow, and Regius Professor of Greek at the time, was nominated to look after Bindon's progress in College, but as things turned out, Longfield hardly ever had any cause for concern.

Following a thorough grinding in the Classics and completion of the minimum statutory year in Arts, Bindon entered the Civil Engineering course to begin a career which was to rise to brilliant heights and be marked by the award of an Honorary Doctorate in later years from his alma mater. As a student in Arts, Bindon showed remarkable talents to the extent that he gained second place overall in the first ranking in Arts in Hilary Term 1846, and first place in the second ranking the following term.

The School of Engineering in the University of Dublin had been established by the Board of Trinity College in November 1841, in response to the need for an increase in the numbers of qualified engineers at a time of considerable expansion in the world economy. The course was introduced 'with the view of combining, as far as is practicable, the theoretical and practical instruction requisite for the Profession of Civil Engineering, and of imparting to the Members of that Profession the other advantages of academical education'.

When Bindon began his studies in the School of Engineering, Professor John (later Sir John) Macneill, the first holder of any Chair of Civil (Practical) Engineering in Ireland, had been barely four years in office and was busy designing and superintending the construction of many miles of main line railways and other works in Ireland and elsewhere. The Great Southern & Western Railway was opened to Carlow in 1846 and the first section of the Midland Great Western Railway to Mullingar in 1847.

With Macneill's preoccupation with railway design and construction, it seems unlikely that he can have devoted much of his time to the Trinity Engineering School, much of the organisation of courses being left to other members of his staff and Bindon therefore, probably saw little of his Professor of Practical Engineering.

One of the first pupils to be accepted by Macneill was James Barton, later to become his assistant in his consulting practice and Engineer-in-Charge of the construction of the River Boyne Railway Viaduct. Stoney was to become Resident Engineer (1854-55) on the Boyne contract under Barton and during his time at Drogheda to develop his theories on diagonal strains (stresses) in lattice girders. His experiences at Drogheda inspired him some years later to complete a definitive two volume work on the Theory of Strains in Girders and Similar Structures.

Macneill was fortunate in having a very able assistant in Trinity in the person of Samuel Downing. Downing was appointed Assistant to the Professor of Civil Engineering in 1847 as Stoney was entering the second year of his three year course in engineering. Downing was the earliest of the academically trained engineers to teach at Trinity, having studied Arts in Trinity and then Natural Philosophy at Edinburgh. This was in contrast to Macneill and his contemporaries who had studied under the master and apprentice system, the only method of acquiring an engineering training in England up until about the third decade of the 19th century. Having completed his course in Edinburgh, Downing became assistant to a contractor in Northampton. Later, he was appointed Resident Engineer for various schemes, including a number of bridges and a viaduct. It is said that he was an excellent lecturer and administrator and was undoubtedly a great influence on the young Stoney. Samuel Downing was later to succeed Macneill and occupy the Chair of Civil Engineering for all of thirty years. Indeed, the year in which Downing eventually retired, Bindon Blood Stoney received his Honorary Doctorate from the University of Dublin. It is a reasonable assumption that Downing was instrumental in persuading the Board and Senate to bestow this well merited award on such an eminent member of the engineering profession. Bindon revelled in his engineering studies. From the records it may be seen that he obtained full marks in all his courses, with the exception of some of the more theoretical courses in his first engineering year. In addition to his Diploma, he was awarded Certificates for 'superior answering' in Practical Engineering, Mechanics & Experimental Physics, and Chemistry & Geology. Thus ended Stoney's academic career and he left college to make his name as an engineer.

Bindon revelled in his engineering studies. From the records it may be seen that he obtained full marks in all his courses, with the exception of some of the more theoretical courses in his first engineering year.

Prof. Samuel Downing (1811-1882); School of Engineering, Trinity College, Dublin

The young engineer

Assistant to an Earl

Family affairs rendered it difficult, if not impossible, for the young Stoney to follow up his University course in the usual manner by serving a term of apprenticeship to some distinguished engineer. Instead, in June 1850, he commenced his working life by taking the place of his elder brother, George Johnstone Stoney, as Assistant Astronomer to the Third Earl of Rosse in the Observatory at Parsonstown (now Birr) in county Offaly.

Following the disastrous famine of 1847, the Earl had resumed construction of the 72" Reflecting Telescope, known as the 'Great Leviathan', in the castle grounds, and Birr had become an important centre for the study of the nebulae, the planets and the moon. The Earl, who was made a Fellow of the Royal Society in 1831 and was its President from 1849 to 1854, began observations in earnest in 1848. Stoney, who was studying engineering at Trinity College Dublin at the time, cannot have failed to have been impressed and excited by the happenings at Birr, just down the road from his birth place at Oakley Park.

Though a considerable amount of the work was connected with the planets, especially Jupiter, the main concentration was on studies of nebulae. Herschel had been able to see these with his telescope and had himself speculated on the possibility that they might be galaxies, or star systems, outside and altogether separate from our own. However, he had not been able to detect their spiral forms and it was reserved for the Birr telescope to make this vital discovery, a discovery which led directly to the conclusion, later to be proved correct, that these galaxies may be at least as numerous as the 100,000 million stars, or suns, which compose our own.

Sir Howard Grubb, in his memoir of Bindon Stoney published in the Proceedings of the Royal Society, remarked that Stoney made his mark by the excellence of the astronomical work he accomplished, and especially by making more accurate delineations of nebulae than had before been obtained, and which continued to be among the best until, at a subsequent period, all eye observations were superseded by photography. One of Stoney's significant achievements was ascertaining by eye observations the spiral character of the great Nebula in Andromeda. He was also responsible for drawing the central portion of the Nebula in Orion.

The 4th Earl of Rosse (then Lord Oxmanton), in his 1867 paper to the Royal Irish Academy, stated that he had every confidence in his observers, who 'had thoroughly mastered the instrument and the methods of observing before they recorded a single independent observation; they were, besides, eminently cautious and painstaking.' As W.Valentine Ball remarked in his 'Reminiscences and Letters of Sir Robert Ball' (1915), Stoney had the essential qualities of accuracy and scientific enthusiasm. It is recorded that some of the observations were made at Birr in temperatures of minus 10degC so it is no wonder that the Earl employed fit young men for the task! In 1852 Stoney decided to look for employment more suited to his engineering qualifications and resigned his post as Assistant at Birr.

Lord Rosse's great 72-inch (1.828m) diameter reflecting telescope of 1845, called the Leviathan of Parsonstown. Mounted between two brick walls, it could move only in a north-south direction

One of Stoney's significant achievements was ascertaining by eye observations the spiral character of the great Nebula in Andromeda. He was also responsible for drawing the central portion of the Nebula in Orion.

Spanish railways

Following a short period of temporary employment, Stoney obtained his first professional engagement, leaving for Spain to join the staff of Greene, an English railway engineer, working on the laying out of the Aranjuez to Almansa Railway south of Madrid. The railway from Madrid had been opened as far as Aranjuez (the junction for the Toledo branch) in February of the previous year. The line was built to a gauge of six Castillian feet, (about 5 feet 6 inches or 1.671 metres), as had been recommended in the 1844 report prepared on behalf of the Spanish government by engineers Subercase and Santa Cruz. Stoney's notebook contains a copy of the agreement dated 10th December, 1851, between Don Jose Salamanca of the Ministry of Public Works and the Government for the building of the Aranjuez to Almansa line and the subsequent conditions under which royal assent was given for construction to commence. The single line railway was to be built in three years in accordance with the terms of the royal decree of 31st December, 1844. Whereas the cuttings and embankments were to accommodate only a single line, all 'works of art' were to be wide enough for two lines, presumably a reference to bridges, to allow for later doubling of the line.

Although launched firmly on a civil engineering career, Bindon maintained his close connections with the Parson's family and later advised the Fourth Earl in the matter of the construction of the mechanical and structural parts of large telescopes.

The Boyne Viaduct

The episode which first brought Stoney to the attention of the engineering profession and the general public began on the banks of the river Boyne at Drogheda. Planned as the link between the then Dublin & Drogheda Railway and the extension northwards from Drogheda connecting with the Ulster Railway at Portadown, the Boyne railway viaduct crosses the estuary of the river Boyne at Drogheda in county Louth, about 32 miles north of Dublin.

The Admiralty requirement, as at the Menai Straits between Anglesey and the North Wales coast, was for a headroom of 90 feet and a minimum clear waterway of 250 feet. To meet these conditions, Sir John MacNeill, the Consultant to the Dublin Belfast Junction Railway Company, suggested constructing the bridge from large wrought-iron lattice girders, connected together in such a way as to create, in effect, a form of tubular bridge. Following a series of tests conducted by James Barton, Macneill's assistant and Chief Engineer to the railway, Macneill developed the design concepts and Barton was given responsibility for the final design drawings.

Work commenced on this major engineering project in May, 1851, but was seriously delayed due to the difficulty in attaining a firm foundation for the northern river pier. The contractor, Evans declared insolvency and the pier in question was eventually finished by the railway company. A temporary bridge, utilising the timber scaffolding, was provided to allow trains to run through to Dublin for the Great Industrial Exhibition of 1853, but as yet the erection of the iron superstructure had not commenced. At this stage Barton looked around for a reliable assistant to supervise the erection work and Stoney, recently returned from his work on Spanish railways, was selected. Thus, at the still tender age of 25 years, Bindon Stoney began work on what was to become regarded as one of the engineering triumphs of the age.

Temporary bridge across the Boyne to allow people to travel to the Dublin Exhibition of 1853

PLATE IV.

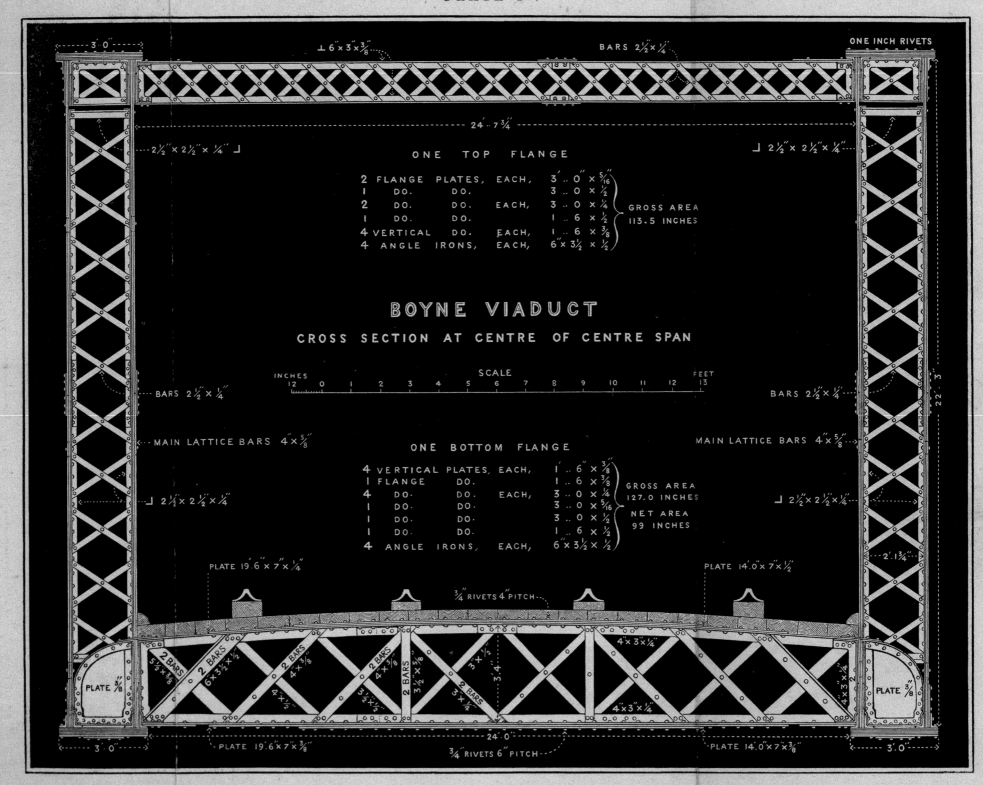

ONE INCH RIVETS

BARS 2½ × ¼

⊥ 6" × 3 × ⅜"

3'·0"

24'·7¾"

2½" × 2½" × ¼ ⌐   ⌐ 2½" × 2½" × ¼"

ONE TOP FLANGE

2 FLANGE PLATES, EACH,   3'·0" × 5⁄16"
1   DO.   DO.   3·0 × ½
2   DO.   DO.   EACH,   3·0 × ¼   } GROSS AREA
1   DO.   DO.   1·6 × ½   113.5 INCHES
4 VERTICAL DO.   EACH,   1·6 × ⅜
4 ANGLE IRONS,   EACH,   6" × 3½ × ½

BOYNE VIADUCT

CROSS SECTION AT CENTRE OF CENTRE SPAN

SCALE

INCHES 12 0   1   2   3   4   5   6   7   8   9 10 11 12 FEET 13

BARS 2½ × ¼   BARS 2½ × ¼

MAIN LATTICE BARS 4" × 5⁄8"   MAIN LATTICE BARS 4" × 5⁄8"

ONE BOTTOM FLANGE

4 VERTICAL PLATES, EACH,   1'·6" × ⅜"
1 FLANGE   DO.   1·6 × ⅜   }
4   DO.   DO.   EACH,   3·0 × ¼   GROSS AREA
1   DO.   DO.   3·0 × 5⁄16   127.0 INCHES
1   DO.   DO.   3·0 × ½   NET AREA
1   DO.   DO.   1·6 × ½   99 INCHES
4 ANGLE IRONS,   EACH,   6" × 3½ × ½ }

⌐ 2½" × 2½" × ¼"   ⌐ 2½" × 2½" × ¼"

22'·3"

2'·1¾"

PLATE 19.6" × 7" × ¼"   PLATE 14.0" × 7" × ½"

PLATE ⅜"   PLATE ⅜"

¾" RIVETS 4" PITCH

3'·0"   3'·0"

PLATE 19.6" × 7" × ⅜"   PLATE 14.0" × 7" × ⅜"

24'·0"

¾" RIVETS 6" PITCH

Dublin Port Chief Engineers
Bindon Blood Stoney (1828-1909)

The viaduct is about 1760 feet in length, and comprised in its original form latticed girders over the three river spans, two of 141 feet and one of 267 feet between bearings, and fifteen semi-circular masonry arch spans, twelve on the south side of the river and three on the north side, each of 60 foot span, all supported on massive masonry piers, mostly founded on rock. The main girders were double-web multiple intersection latticed type, continuous over the piers, whilst the cross girders were single-web double intersection latticed type. The principle of multiple-lattice construction in wrought-iron was first applied on a large scale in the Boyne Viaduct and resulted in a significant increase in the knowledge of the structural properties and behaviour under load of wrought-iron.

The Boyne Viaduct was the first of its kind in which, upon a large scale, the strength of each part was accurately proportioned to the stress it had to withstand. This saved material and, by reducing the weight, avoided all unnecessary stresses that were a feature of earlier viaducts. The safety of the structure was increased, as well as the length of span which could be achieved. In the Queen's College in Galway, Professor Blood had carried out a very elegant analysis of the stresses in continuous girders in three spans. This Stoney successfully applied to the calculation of the points of inflexion of the Boyne Viaduct girders.

The original viaduct was an object of great interest amongst contemporary engineers and is mentioned in several works on engineering practice of the day, notably in Stoney's 'Theory of Strains in Girders and Similar Structures', first published in 1866-69 in two volumes.

Stoney set down in his notebook the reasons for preferring lattice beams to plate girders, viz:

– Economy of material in the sides;
– Certainty of calculation, parts being exactly proportional to strain (stress);
– Smaller surface exposed to wind;
– Capability of applying cast-iron in place of more expensive material; and
– Capability of cutting top or bottom chords in 'continuous' (or suspended) beams, etc., which could not be done in tubular bridges.

The notebook also contains details of the larch and beech centring employed for the Boyne Viaduct arches and a full description of the loading tests carried out on the masonry piers, one of the 24 foot roadway beams, the pillar test, and the preliminary and official tests of the completed structure.

The test conducted for the Railway Inspectorate consisted of running an engine, tender and first class coach of the Dublin-Drogheda Railway Co. across the viaduct at both fast and slow speeds. Deflections at centre span were very small and the structure passed the tests with flying colours.

A pillar test was carried out to ascertain whether the arrangement of bracing being used in the structure would enable a bar, thin in proportion to its length, to sustain an end pressure approaching the crushing weight of the iron. Accordingly, an experimental beam, similar to those used at the centre of the centre span of the viaduct, was constructed under Barton's directions, and erected in the midst of some timber scaffolding which had been used as an hoist during the construction of the masonry piers.

As a result of this and other experiments, Stoney concluded that 'The strongest form of rectangular cell to resist compression as a pillar, is one in which the chief part of the material is collected at the angles, leaving only so much material in the sides as is requisite to hold the angle pillars in the direction of the thrust.'

The last rivet on the Boyne Viaduct was ceremoniously driven by Barton and Stoney on the 27th March, 1855, the viaduct having been opened for light traffic some weeks earlier. A few months later, Stoney moved back to Dublin to take up an appointment as Assistant Engineer to George Halpin in Dublin Port.

Opposite page:
Boyne Viaduct:
Cross Section at centre
of Centre Span

Right:
Boyne Viaduct as
completed in 1855

The principle of multiple-lattice construction in wrought-iron was first applied on a large scale in the Boyne Viaduct and resulted in a significant increase in the knowledge of the structural properties and behaviour under load of wrought-iron.

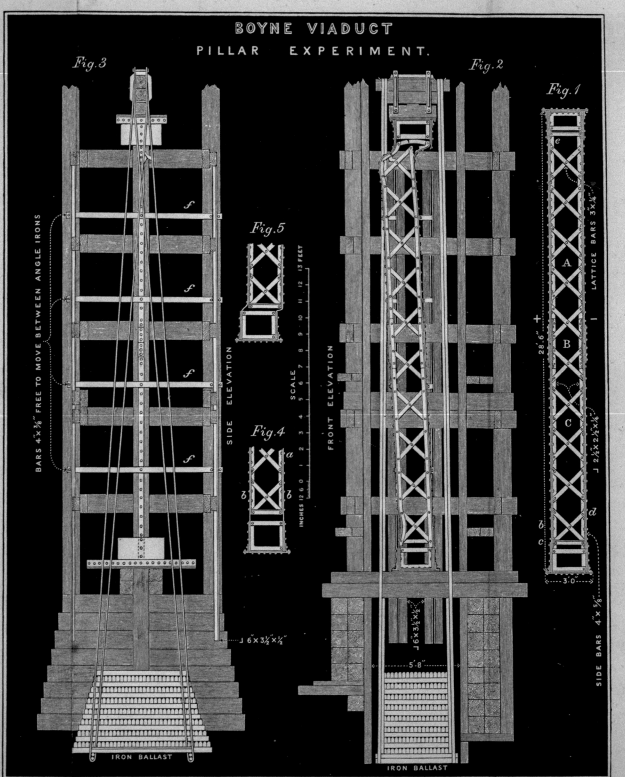

The last rivet on the Boyne Viaduct was ceremoniously driven by Barton and Stoney on the 27th March, 1855, the viaduct having been opened for light traffic some weeks earlier. A few months later, Stoney moved back to Dublin to take up an appointment as Assistant Engineer to George Halpin in Dublin Port.

Planning the future
of the port

Stoney's appointment

Prior to 1867, the Corporation for Preserving and Improving the Port of Dublin, commonly called the Ballast Board, was responsible, not only for the Harbour and Port of Dublin, but for the lighthouses around the coasts of Ireland.

By the mid 1850's, there was a significant increase in activity in Dublin Port due to the improvement of conditions at the Bar resulting from the work of George Halpin I on the North Bull Wall and the general increase in world trading. Work on land reclamation and the construction of a graving dock had commenced and George Halpin II (who had succeeded his father in 1854) found it increasingly difficult as Inspector of Works to combine his responsibilities for maintaining and improving the lighthouse service with his duties in the port. His Assistant, Thomas Ramsey, resigned and, in January, 1856, the Board advertised for an Assistant to the Inspector of Works.

The Board received no fewer than 73 applications for the position, reflecting both the prestige attached to the job and the increasing availability of qualified personnel. The five selected were J. Long, Walmesley Stanley, Joseph Green, John Ramsey (apparently no relation to the outgoing assistant engineer) and BINDON BLOOD STONEY.

As a result of the Committee's recommendation, the Board was specially summoned for Friday, 22nd February and the five candidates duly examined. On proceeding to a ballot, the Board voted as follows: J.Ramsey 9, J.Long 5, B.B.Stoney 2, J.Green 1 and W.Stanley 1.

The names of Ramsey and Long were further balloted for, John Ramsey emerging a 7 to 2 winner. He was duly elected as Assistant to the Engineer of the Port of Dublin at a salary of £250 per annum. Stoney was it seemed not to figure in the future development of the port after all!

The Board being a Public Body, the appointment of Ramsey was sent, as was the practice, to the Lord Lieutenant for his approval. Ramsey, however, had other ideas. He kept the Board in a state of uncertainty by delaying his acceptance of the position. Finally, on 10th April, in a letter to Lees, the Secretary to the Board, Ramsey delivered his bombshell. Writing from Newry, he explained that, having been 21 years with the Newry Navigation Company, he could not leave them without at least six months notice. Ramsey went on to say that, as he could not bring himself to part with them upon any but the most friendly terms, he had no alternative but to resign his appointment as Assistant Engineer to the Ballast Board.

The Board was once again summoned to meet to proceed to appoint a replacement for Ramsey, Greene and Walmsley Stanley being informed that their attendance would not be required, a polite way of saying that they had been unsuccessful!

On the 25th April, the Board duly met, the record of the meeting showing that 'When proceeding to a ballot it appeared that Mr Bindon B.Stoney (one of the five candidates previously selected out of the entire number of applicants as most eligible, on the occasion of Mr Ramsey's appointment) was duly elected at a salary of £250 per annum.' Stoney was in and his career and reputation were thereafter to be made in harbour work. His name in time became known to the majority of Dubliners and was synonymous with the creation of a deep-water port for the City of Dublin, a facility which was ultimately to benefit the whole country.

At the time of his appointment, Bindon lived with his widowed mother, sisters Anne and Kate, and his elder brother George Johnstone, in the family home at Number 89, a fine house at the Morehampton Road end of Waterloo Road in Dublin. Whilst George travelled to work in Dublin Castle, Bindon made his way each morning to his office in the Ballast Board building in Westmoreland Street.

A postcard view of the River Liffey, Dublin, published by (John) Evelyn Leslie Wrench from 1900-1904

Stoney's name in time became known to the majority of Dubliners and was synonymous with the creation of a deep-water port for the City of Dublin, a facility which was ultimately to benefit the whole country.

The Graving Dock

I n the 1840's and 1850's, the growing demand for improved berthage along the river frontage had led to the construction of timber wharves in front of the north quays. (This was in order that vessels could be berthed away from the shallow areas adjacent to the quay side). It had also become evident that the existing repair slips were far from adequate and plans were duly laid for the provision of a large graving dock.

In order to accommodate the latest mail steamers, it was agreed initially that the dock should be 400 feet long and 70 feet wide (It was eventually built 80 feet wide). William Dargan, the eminent railway contractor, began work in 1853, the project taking seven years to complete.

The appointment of Stoney in 1856 as Assistant Engineer relieved Halpin of much of the day to day work in the port and, as a consequence, Stoney became in effect Acting Port Engineer. As such, he supervised the later stages of construction of the graving dock, acting as Resident Engineer. In 1859 he was made Executive Engineer to the Board and authorised to sign accounts 'to release Halpin for more important purposes.'

The new graving dock, opened on 9 February, 1860, was, according to a contemporary account in The Engineer of 8 February, 1867, '...one of the most excellent specimens of material and workman-ship...'. The design for the graving dock is, of course, attributed to George Halpin II, Inspector of Works, whom Stoney was to succeed in 1862, but there seems little doubt that Stoney quickly struck up a good working relationship with Dargan, which was reflected in the excellent workmanship, particularly the masonry work. The entrance gates to the dock were designed to the joint patent of Wyld and Mallet, and were built in Dublin by the firm of J.& R.Mallet at the Victoria Foundry. They were similar to those at Limerick and gave excellent service. Stoney, however, had to counter problems with the pumping arrangements for emptying the dock, skilfully resolving the problems to the extent that it was possible to completely empty the dock in around four hours on a 13 foot tide. It is worth noting that the dock, which was built at a cost of £116,704, including the adjoining repair shed, operated practically continuously until 1989, when it was taken out of service due to the bad condition of the gates. Mallet's original gates installed in 1860 were renewed in 1881 and again in 1931.

In 1858, Stoney was asked to report on and prepare an estimate of costs for the construction of an Eastern breakwater. The report, dated 12 March, 1858, was referred by the Board to Halpin for his opinion as to the form of contract. The breakwater was needed to protect Halpin's Pond from the effects of easterly gales. Construction began east of the No.1 graving dock shortly after the dock was completed. Stoney was able to try out some of his ideas by building about 1100 feet of the E-W wall in concrete. By July, 1868, the wall had been extended some 450 feet to the south to form an L- shaped breakwater (See map).

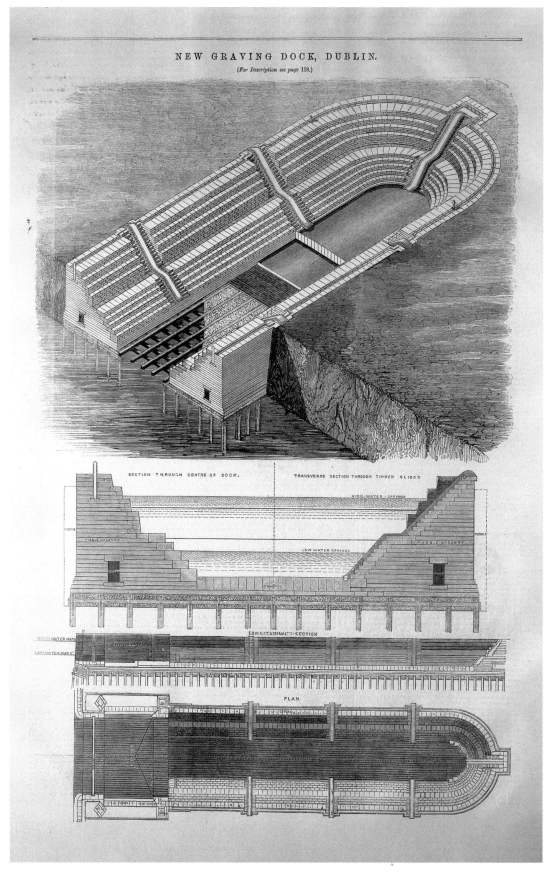

**Dublin No.1 Graving Dock
as built in 1860**

Planning Alexandra Basin

In January, 1861, Stoney presented a preliminary report to the Harbour Improvement Committee which contained proposals for the creation of a basin or wet dock east of the then extremity of the North Quays. He also proposed a complete reorganisation of the dredging operations in the port. With regard to the latter, Stoney considered that the best solution was to convey the mud in hopper floats and dump the contents in deep water off Howth, east of the Bailey Lighthouse. The alternatives involved continuing to dump on Sandymount Strand as hitherto, or on the North Bull. One of the leading English harbour engineers at the time, James Walker, agreed with Stoney's views, provided hoppers suitable for towing out to sea could be provided.

Stoney's brief had been to propose how best to provide additional accommodation for shipping to meet the increasing prosperity of the port and to provide new opportunities for increased trade. Any design was to be seen as part of a long-term plan and was required to harmonise with the existing facilities. In his report, Stoney laid great stress on the necessity for building for the future. He felt that it was far wiser to proceed less rapidly and more solidly, thus enabling the Port of Dublin 'to compete with the other great ports of the United Kingdom.'

The constant expense of underpinning existing quay walls to prevent collapse, and the provision of timber wharves along the line of the quays highlighted the need to take the long-term view by constructing substantial deep-water quays to meet the demands of the increasing overseas trade.

To avoid the heavy cost of temporary works when carrying out engineering work below tide levels, Stoney proposed constructing large monolithic masonry concrete blocks on 'terra firma' and transporting them to their planned location using a massive floating crane or shears float. Each block was to be placed on a levelled foundation, prepared by hand by labourers working under compressed air from within a diving bell.

In his initial report, Stoney proposed providing a depth of 20 feet LWOST (Low Water Ordinary Spring Tides) on the inner or northern face and 16 feet LWOST on the outer or river face of an Extension to the North Wall Quays. These depths were subsequently increased to 24 feet and 22 feet respectively, indicating perhaps that even Stoney could be conservative or that, on the other hand, ship size and draft increased at a greater rate than had been predicted.

This draft plan contained a proposal to angle the entrance to the basin, in much the same manner as the present-day Ocean Pier, in order to better facilitate the entry and exit of vessels using the Basin. The basin was designed to enclose a little over 47 acres with an internal quay line of about one mile, the initial estimated cost of the project being £350,000.

During the first half of 1862, Stoney worked on a number of drafts of his proposals culminating in the detailed Plan No.4 which was presented to the Committee on 10th August. Halpin had been rather put out when Stoney had, in his absence, presented the Committee with his preliminary report, containing as it did proposals of such major importance to the future of the port. He disagreed totally with Stoney as to the best method of attaining the objectives and countered by setting down his own proposals together with a detailed list of plant and equipment required to build what he referred to in his report as the 'New Tidal Docks Port of Dublin.' Halpin's report is dated 3 August and the List of Plant 5 August, predating Stoney's Plan No. 4 by a few days.

Significantly, and some may say predictably, Halpin signed his report George Halpin/Engineer/Inspector of Works, instead of just Inspector of Works, as if to remind his junior colleague of his position. Stoney must have been well aware that Halpin was preparing his own set of proposals and he set about developing his own plans for the new floating basin and drawing the attention of the Committee to experience elsewhere of the use of large masses of masonry concrete for harbour work.

Having considered Stoney's Plan No. 4, Halpin wrote to the Committee pouring cold water on the proposals and urging the Committee to adopt the more traditional method of quay wall construction involving building the quay walls within coffer dams. He also did not believe that the construction and placing of such large blocks was feasible. In the face of this criticism of his professional opinion from Halpin who, although in failing health, still held the senior engineering position in the Port, Stoney replied at length in a supplementary report dated 24 August. Stoney calculated that Halpin's proposals and method of working, if carried out would at least double the cost and would take considerably longer to execute. He also doubted whether timber of the requisite length could be procured at reasonable cost for such large and deep coffer dams.

From an examination of Stoney's Plan No. 4, we learn that he proposed to first build an embankment running east of the Graving Dock together with a sloping or angled eastern breakwater. A reclaimed area to the east of the Graving Dock was to be the site of a timber wharf on which the large monolithic blocks for the new quays were to be built. The North Quays would then be extended gradually as finance permitted, by laying the blocks on prepared foundations, the substantial associated dredging of river and basin being carried out as required by the progress of the project.

In addition to the details of how he proposed to carry out the projects, Stoney went to considerable lengths to convince the Committee that Halpin's criticisms were ill-founded. Firstly, the placing of concrete blocks under water had been successfully carried in France and elsewhere; secondly, that it had been proven that Portland cement concrete was superior to Pozzolano or lime concrete, then in common use; thirdly, that, although the largest concrete blocks moved from place to place were, up to that time, no more than 50 tons in weight, considerably larger masses of concrete had been formed; and lastly, that moving the large blocks should not be that difficult, given that heavier masses were frequently raised utilising the buoyant action of water.

The Committee and the Board were convinced by Stoney's arguments and proceeded to lay plans to raise the necessary finance in order to commence the preliminary work and acquire the heavy plant needed to undertake the project. Halpin, his health failing, decided to retire.

Dublin Port 1856

1 Essex Bridge	**5** Inner Dock	**9** Pigeon House Harbour	**14** No.1 Graving Slip
2 Liffey Bridge	**6** George's Dock	**10** Poolbeg Lighthouse	**15** No.2 Graving Slip
3 Carlisle Bridge	**7** Steam Packet Wharf	**11** North Bull Lighthouse	**16** Dockyard
4 Timber Wharves, North Quays	*(Gross Berth)*	**12** Inland Breakwater	
	8 South Quays	**13** Halpin's Pond	

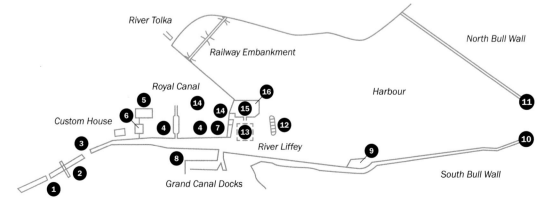

Worker welfare

Stoney always took a great interest in the welfare of his workers, but he was also determined to promote the most efficient working of the Port. After taking over as Chief Engineer from Halpin in 1862, he wrote to the Board from the Engineer's Office in the Ballast Office (The Engineer's Office moved to the North Wall in 1867) as follows: 'I have the honour to lay before the Committee a list of fourteen elderly and inefficient labourers whom I think it would be expedient to pension off or get rid of by donations. I believe when the pension is 3/-, or upwards per week, it would be more beneficial than a donation, as it makes the relatives take an interest in the old pensioner, whereas the donation is often gone in a few weeks and the labourer is then forced to go into the poorhouse.'

Stoney then detailed the cost of pensioning off these unproductive labourers (representing about 5% of the workforce at the time) and concluded by giving as his opinion that 'these are comparatively small sums of money to pay for increased efficiency and they will be fully repaid by greater activity and energy in the works, besides acting as an encouragement to steadiness and attention to business.' The Board's response was to ask Stoney to prepare a detailed report on Pensions and Charities as applying in the Port and to comment on the existing arrangements for relief of sick and superannuated labourers, including all workmen under the rank of tradesmen.

Stoney found that the practice up to that time had been that in certain cases of very long service (35 years and upwards) a small pension rarely exceeding 5/- per week was granted when old age and infirmity rendered the recipient unfit for further work. In cases of lesser service, payment of one to two guineas for a period of four weeks was sometimes awarded which, if the illness continued, was repeated at intervals, becoming in effect a modified pension. In the case of death in service, the only benefit was generally a donation of two guineas made towards the funeral expenses.

Stoney felt that when men were unable to work for short or even extended periods due to sickness, there were a number of charitable organisations in the city set up for the express purpose of assisting them and their dependents. He proposed that the donations paid to workers on sick leave be discontinued and that the limited funds available be applied instead to placing old and infirm workers on the pension list. He proposed a new scale of donations and pensions which essentially gave lump sums to workers leaving after less than 15 years service and an increasing scale of pensions for years of service in excess of 15, up to a maximum pension of 5/- per week after 50 years service. As Stoney's proposals were calculated not to increase the financial burden on the Board in the medium term, these eminently practical proposals were accepted and Stoney was entrusted with their implementation.

In the area of industrial relations, Stoney's proposals were ahead of their time, being considered profoundly humane when compared with the treatment meted out to employees elsewhere at that time. The following year Stoney again showed his interest in the well-being of his staff by suggesting to the Board that they finance the establishment of a small library of technical books for the use of his foremen in order that they might better themselves.

Above:
The various homes of Bindon Blood Stoney in Dublin 4, including 63 Wellington Road; 89 Waterloo Road; 40/42 Wellington Road and 14 Elgin Road

Left:
North and South Quays, Sir John Rogerson Quay, Dublin 2

Quay reconstruction

Acting on the instructions of the Harbour Improvement Committee, Stoney reported in 1865 on improvement works in the Port either then in progress or planned. He considered that the most pressing need was to provide deep-water berths along the South Quays and that the approaches to the quays should be dredged to at least the depth at the Bar, or about 14 feet below LWOST. A case was also made for a second graving dock, but the dock was, in the event, not built until the 1950's owing to the decline in demand for ship repair and maintenance facilities. The floating gate idea, first suggested by Stoney, was used in the No. 2 Graving Dock.

At the time of Stoney's proposals, 392 feet of Burgh Quay was being rebuilt under the direction of a young Resident Engineer, Isaac. J. Mann, the quay having been on the point of collapsing into the river due to a build-up of water pressure behind the quay wall occasioned by inadequate drainage provision. The contractor, John C.Morris, began work in July, 1865, and the work was completed the following April.

The rebuilding and deepening of the eastern end of the North Wall Quay, commenced using direct labour in 1864, was completed in 1869. By the completion of the work, berths varying from 16 feet to 18 feet at LWOST were obtained and were in great demand by large vessels, which hitherto had been subject to the heavy expense of lightening in Kingstown (now Dun Laoghaire), or in the river, in order to proceed to their berths.

By 1866, the Ballast Board having become somewhat financially embarrassed, asked Stoney to find ways of curbing expenditure. Progress was slowed on the build-up of the plant required for the projected North Wall Basin Project, but contractually nothing much could be done to delay the building and equipping of the major items, some of which had already been delivered.

On the domestic front, Bindon's family had moved in 1864 to a recently built house at 63 Wellington Road. Two years later Bindon moved across the road to No. 42 and, in the same year, his brother George moved into the house next door, No. 40. It seems that his mother and sisters continued to live at No. 63, and a Miss Stoney is recorded as living there until 1929.

In 1869, the newly constituted Dublin Port & Docks Board, having had their application for a Public Works Loan to construct a second graving dock and deepen 1000 feet of Sir John Rogerson's Quay turned down, nevertheless decided to proceed with the quay deepening on the basis that the surplus revenue generated by the port would be sufficient to meet the cost of construction.

The contract for the rebuilding of Sir John Rogerson's Quay was awarded to William J. Doherty. Doherty, who was a civil engineer by profession, and a member of the Institution, had gained extensive experience, whilst on the engineering staff of William McCormick, of the construction of what were then amongst the largest coffer-dams in England. These included that across the entrance to the Low-Water Basin at Birkenhead Docks, and those at the Victoria Dock Extension and the West Dock at Hull. In the summer of 1869, Stoney received a tender from Doherty for the removal of the river wall at Sir John Rogerson's Quay, and the erection of a new wall at a greater depth, to be carried out to Stoney's plans and specifications. The foundations of the wall as built in 1820 were only three to four feet below low water and thus practically useless for the size of shipping wishing to use the port, as dredging could not be carried out close to it for fear of endangering the structure.

As no details were given in the specifications, Doherty was responsible for the design of the coffer-dam and fully described its construction in a paper to the Institution of Civil Engineers in 1877, at a time when he was commencing the reconstruction of Carlisle Bridge and preparing the foundations for the Beresford Swing Bridge (See Chapter Six). He describes how, as suitable clay was not available, he initially used peat-moss, brought by canal to Dublin, for puddling (sealing) between the inner and outer walls of the coffer dam. The peat moss answered very well but, when the first section of the old quay wall had been removed and excavation commenced, suitable clay was found in sufficient quantities to use as puddling for the remainder of the contract. All the sand and gravel used was obtained by dredging and extensive use was made of Portland cement and 'one of Mr Stoney's concrete mixers.'

The method of making concrete and mortar adopted by Stoney differed in certain respects from that then in general use. He preferred a rapid mixture of the ballast or sand with cement or lime to the slow 'triturating' (mixing grinding) process of the mortar pan with edge runners. The concrete mixer, designed by Stoney, was driven by a 3 HP engine and had an output of between 10 and 12 cubic yards per hour. The mixer consisted of a fixed horizontal or inclined trough, open on the top, with a longitudinal axis, having stout iron blades at short intervals, which, as they revolved simultaneously 'pugged' (compressed) the materials and screwed them forward. The water was let in gradually through a rose, the first few blades incorporating the materials in a dry state before they encountered the water.

Cross section of North Wall Quay showing positions of old quay walls exposed during reconstruction of quay in 1872

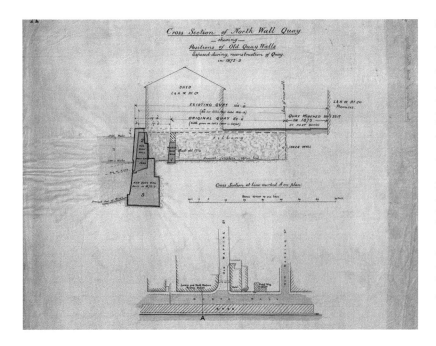

The rebuilding and deepening of the eastern end of the North Wall Quay, commenced using direct labour in 1864, was completed in 1869. By the completion of the work, berths varying from 16 feet to 18 feet at LWOST were obtained and were in great demand by large vessels, which hitherto had been subject to the heavy expense of lightening in Kingstown (now Dun Laoghaire), or in the river, in order to proceed to their berths.

Building the deep-water port

The basin project revived

In 1869, the Board turned its attention once again to the best means of providing additional deep-water dock or quay accommodation to meet the increasing overseas trade of the port.

Having given the subject their fullest consideration, the Board decided to adopt the Report of the Harbour Improvement Committee which recommended proceeding with Stoney's earlier plans for the prolongation of the North Wall. The new quay wall was to be faced on both sides, so as to afford double room tor vessels, the breadth of quay to be not less than twice that of the existing North Wall. An alternative proposal was to provide a new wet dock on the south side of the river, but this was not proceeded with. The Board accordingly instructed Stoney to prepare the necessary plans and specification prior to inviting tenders to have the work carried out by contract.

Stoney had experienced considerable delays in the North Quay deepening work in the late 1860's occasioned by pumps breaking down due to being overworked in trying to keep the water out of the workings. This must have served to strengthen his resolve to build the projected extension to the North Quays by the placing of large pre-constructed masonry blocks rather than the traditional method of working within a dewatered coffer dam.

In 1863, he had conducted tests to assess the relative costs of masonry and concrete work. He arranged for two short 100 foot sections of the retaining wall of the embankment on the north side of the new basin to be built, one section in rubble masonry set in lime mortar, the other in Portland cement concrete. He found that concrete worked out around 50% cheaper for that type of work.

The methods devised by Stoney were in fact to prove very effective and economical. In a report to the British Association for the Advancement of Science, meeting in Dublin in 1878, he reported that there had been annual savings of around £16000, after repaying the capital invested in plant.

The shears float, bell float and diving bell

At the time of the revival of the North Wall Extension Project, the block wharf had already been built and much of the necessary plant acquired, including the shears and bell floats, hopper floats and a steam tug. The design of both the floating shears and the diving bell and pontoon was carried out by Stoney. Design sketches and structural calculations for the shears float are to be found in his notebooks for the early 1860's.

The space on the block wharf being limited, Stoney's plan was to build about 300 feet of quay wall in the first year of the project and then use the space thus created to accommodate the building of further blocks. The rate of block laying in subsequent years was then to double, thereby creating about 600 feet of additional quay wall per annum, depending on available finance.

Harland & Wolff of Belfast were contracted to build the hull of the floating shears, Courtney & Stephens of Dublin supplying the machinery. The shears float was delivered to Dublin in 1866, the final cost being £17,058. Grendon & Co. of Drogheda built the diving bell and its accompanying pontoon, George Strype of that firm designing the horizontal air pump and the air tube passing down the inside of the funnel of the bell. The diving bell now forms the major part of a small interpretative permanent exhibition on Sir John Rogerson's Quay on the south bank of the river.

The section of the hull of the floating shears as built was 48 feet by 48 feet and 14 feet deep. It was also rectangular in plan with the exception of the bow, which was semi-circular. The overall length was 130 feet. A ballast or counter-weight tank at the stern occupied 30 feet, the deck of which was 3 feet higher than the rest of the vessel.

The hull was strengthened by two transverse bulkheads distanced 24 feet from each end. Two double-webbed plate girders, each 3 feet wide by 18 feet deep ran fore and aft from end to end of the hull, dividing it longitudinally into three parts, and distributing the great pressure of the shear legs over the whole length of the vessel, the iron deck and bottom of which acted as flanges to the longitudinal girders. The ends of the hull and the transverse bulkheads also transferred a portion of the shearing strains to the sides, and brought them and the adjoining parts of the deck and bottom plates also into action as girders. Thus the hull could be regarded as a powerful tubular girder with several vertical webs which distributed the shearing strains over its whole area.

Right:
Barge with lifting crane

Far right:
Shears float

Opposite page:
Block Wharf and Block; illustrating Stoney's Paper on Recent Improvements in the Port of Dublin

Plate II.

BLOCK WHARF,

AND

BLOCK.

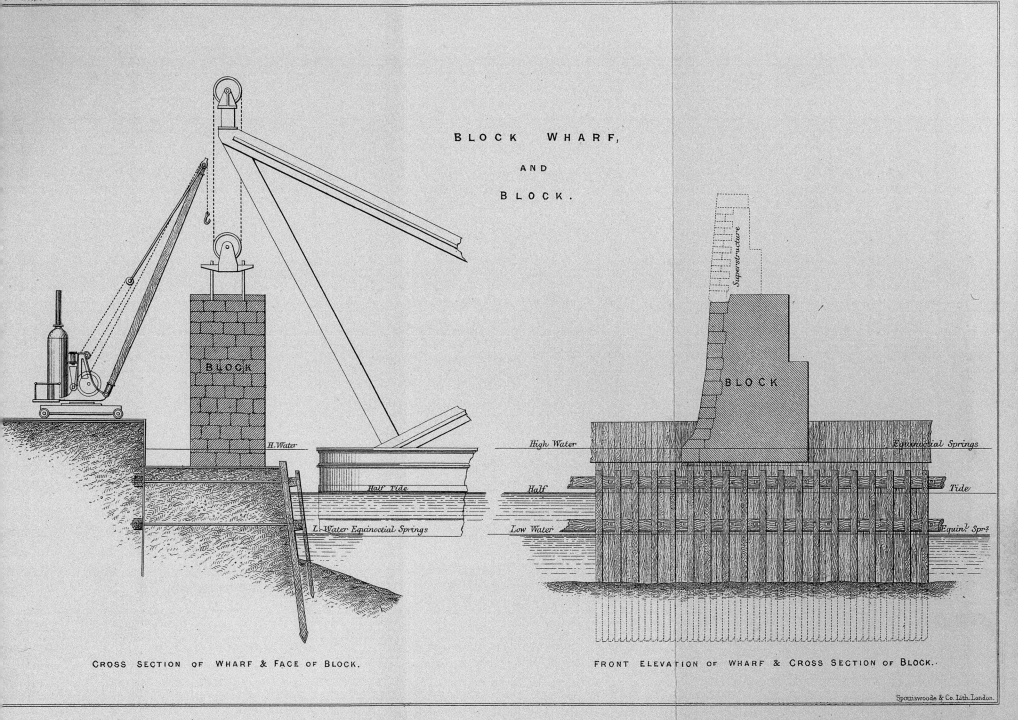

Superstructure

BLOCK

BLOCK

H.Water

Equinoctial Springs

High Water

Half Tide

Half

Tide

L. Water Equinoctial Springs

Low Water

Equin.l Sprs

CROSS SECTION OF WHARF & FACE OF BLOCK.

FRONT ELEVATION OF WHARF & CROSS SECTION OF BLOCK.

Spottiswoode & Co. Lith. London.

Illustrating M.r B. B. Stoney's Paper on Recent Improvements in the Port of Dublin.

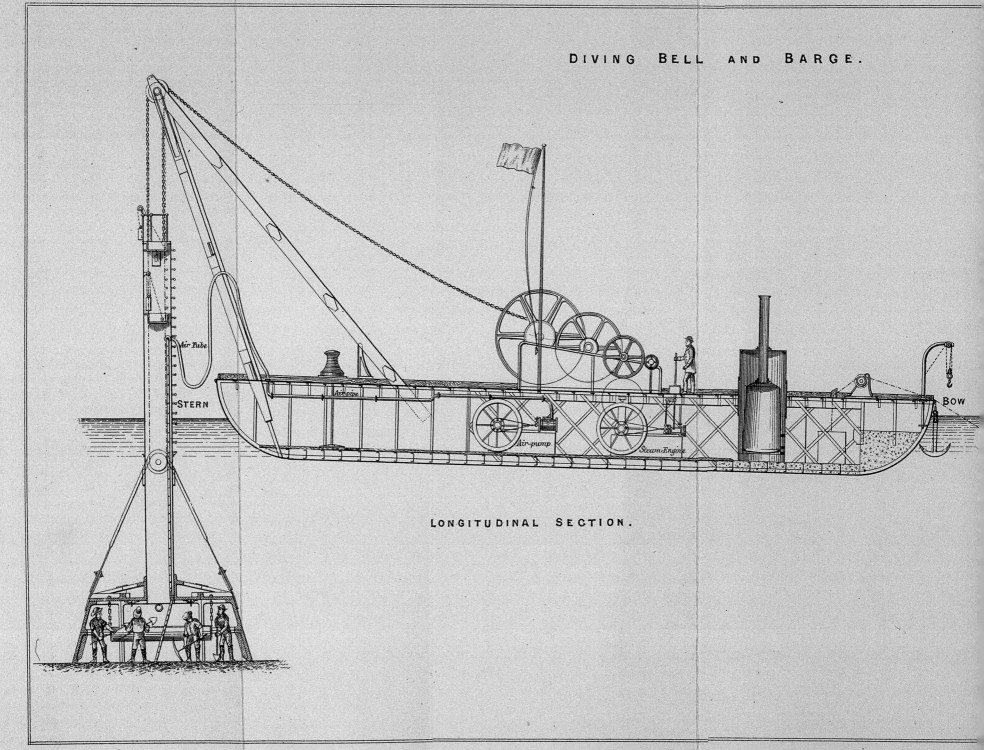

DIVING BELL AND BARGE.

STERN

Air Tube

Air-pipe

Air-pump

Steam-Engine

BOW

LONGITUDINAL SECTION.

Illustrating Mr B. B. Stoney's Paper on Recent Improvements in the Port of

Dublin Port Chief Engineers
Bindon Blood Stoney (1828-1909)

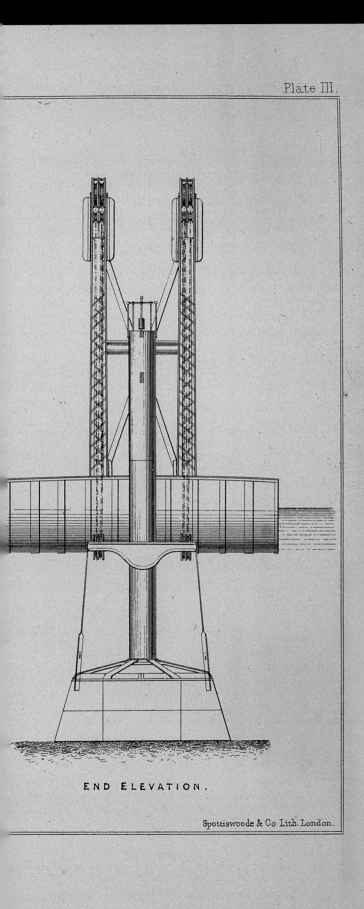

Plate III.

END ELEVATION.

Spottiswoode & Co Lith. London.

The bottom, floors and sides of the hull, bulkheads, etc., were constructed of various thicknesses of wrought iron plate. The tank was 30 feet long by 17 feet deep by 48 feet wide. Considerable amounts of concrete were placed in the bottom of the tank to overcome its displacement when water was pumped out.

The framework above the deck consisted of two pairs of shear legs with powerful backstays reaching diagonally from the top of each pair to the feet of the other. The forward shears supported the block hanging from the chains, those aft supported the tank. The centre of the block was 15 feet from the bow of the vessel and the centre of the tank 15 feet from the stern.

When a block was suspended at one end and water was pumped into the tank and the vessel floated on an even keel, the total weight supported by the hull was twice the weight of the block. Thus, when a block was hanging from the chains, a thrust of 700 tons passed downward through the forward pair of shear legs, tending to punch them through the bottom of the vessel. The vertical component of strain in the second pair of backstays, being in the opposite direction, balanced a considerable part of the downward thrust in the legs, and relieved the great local pressure at their intersection with the deck. All the machinery was driven from a 14 HP horizontal high pressure steam engine.

The diving bell consists of a chamber 16 feet square, 20 feet square at base level, and 6.5 feet high inside, constructed from 25 massive castings, with planed joints, bolted together. From the centre of the roof rises a tube, 3 feet in diameter and 37.5 feet high. The total height of the chamber and tube is 44 feet, which is the limiting depth at which the bell was capable of working. The upper end of the tube forms an air lock 6.5 feet high. The bell weighs 80.5 tons. The bell float was 80 feet in length. 30 feet wide and 8 feet deep, with two longitudinal single webbed girders running fore and aft in the line of the shear legs, the girders being latticed amidships for about half their length and plated at their extremities. A quantity of concrete, at the end remote from the bell, balanced the weight at the other end, and left a safe freeboard at the stern when the bell was out of the water.

The compressed air was cooled by the surrounding water before being fed to the chamber, keeping the air temperature in the chamber to between 50 and 60 degrees F. In practice, it became unbearingly hot on occasions and men could not work for longer than about 30 minutes consecutively. Continuous working required two shifts consisting of a ganger and six men. They worked in an area of 400 square feet, equivalent to the space available in a large living room in a modern house.

Diving Bell and Barge, Longitudinal Section

The diving bell consists of a chamber 16 feet square, 20 feet square at base level, and 6.5 feet high inside, constructed from 25 massive castings, with planed joints, bolted together. From the centre of the roof rises a tube, 3 feet in diameter and 37.5 feet high.

It was possible to begin the work almost immediately as the necessary heavy plant, including the floating shears, diving bell and barge had already been acquired. In addition, the Board had, in 1870, obtained a loan of £150,000 from the Bank of Ireland to pay for the improvements recommended by the Harbour Improvement Committee.

Above:
**Alexandra Basin:
Engineers Office (left) and
Harbour Masters Office
(right)**

Opposite page:
**Views of the diving bell
and barge**

The great work begins

The major undertaking was to build new quay walls to form part of a tidal basin on the northern side of the estuary of the River Liffey. The great cost of temporary works for engineering work below water, especially when foundations are laid within the coffer dams at great depth below the water surface level, had led Stoney to propose using large monolithic blocks, constructed on shore and lifted into position by a floating shears, the foundations first being excavated and levelled by labourers working under compressed air in a diving bell.

It was possible to begin the work almost immediately as the necessary heavy plant, including the floating shears, diving bell and barge had already been acquired. In addition, the Board had, in 1870, obtained a loan of £150,000 from the Bank of Ireland to pay for the improvements recommended by the Harbour Improvement Committee. It was decided to carry out the work by direct labour and not to go to tender, a decision which was to result in the ensuing years in the gradual build-up of a highly skilled labour force in the Port.

The plan was to build an experimental length of some 500 to 600 feet of quay wall, dredged to 22 feet LWOST on the outside, or river face, and 24 feet on the inside and, if all went well, to continue to extend the wall in sections, as finance permitted, without interfering with shipping movements.

As soon as each section of quay wall was completed, the berths provided were to be opened to shipping.

Work commenced on the great project in May of 1871 when the first of the large 350-ton blocks was successfully lifted from its site on the block wharf by the shears float, afterwards being-placed on its prepared bed. Another nine blocks were constructed and laid during the remainder of the year, representing a length of 100 feet of new quay wall. The Board considered that 'the construction of the Quay Wall reflects the highest credit upon their Engineer, Mr Stoney, for having designed and carried into effect, without the slightest accident, so novel and advantageous a work.'

The same year saw the appointment of John Purser Griffith as Stoney's Assistant. Griffith, the son of a distinguished Congregational Minister, was born in 1848 beside the harbour at Holyhead in North Wales. His imagination must have been stirred by the enterprise of the men who built the great breakwater at Holyhead and he turned to the field of civil engineering, coming to Dublin to study in the Engineering School at Trinity College. He graduated in 1868 and, after an initial year of experience with Antrim County Council, joined Stoney in the task of developing the deep-water port of Dublin.

Dublin Port Chief Engineers
Bindon Blood Stoney (1828-1909)

Laying the massive blocks

The heart of each block comprised stones each up to two tons in weight placed on their ends or edges, the voids being filled with 7:1 Ballast/ Cement concrete and small stones rammed in to compact the mass. Two 11cwt cast-iron girders were built into the base of each block to spread the load from the wrought iron suspender bars, which in turn supported the block and were themselves connected to the lifting chains.

Each block reached from 24 feet below to 3 feet above LWOST. They were 21 feet 4 inches wide at the base and 12 feet long in the direction of the wall. The cubic volume of each block was 5000 cu. ft. giving a maximum weight of around 350 tons. The outer face of each block next to the shipping was formed of Dublin Calp limestone facestones set in a 4:1 sand:cement mortar.

The upper portion of the wall above low water mark was built in the normal way and faced with granite ashlar, coped with granite blocks each of two to four tons weight. The total height was 42 feet 10 inches. Vertical grooves, 3 feet wide and 18 inches deep were formed in the sides of each block. When the blocks were placed side by side, the grooves were filled up with concrete to provide a key between adjacent blocks.

The blocks were built on a timber wharf, specifically built for the purpose, 461 feet long and about one-third of a mile from the quay wall site. The blocks generally took three to four weeks to build and could be moved after ten weeks of curing and hardening. The operation of lifting and setting a block was as follows:

The floating shears was brought bow-on to the block wharf during the flood tide, and the lifting chains attached to the iron suspending bars passing through each block. The chains were then hauled in by the winches on board, and water pumped into the large tanks at the after-end of the vessel to counterbalance the weight of the block, which was then floated to its destination and lowered into place during the following period of low water. Special arrangements were provided for spreading the load when lifting the blocks.

The work of block laying for quay walls required extreme accuracy to secure closeness of the joints and the correct direction of the wall. To ensure these results, it was necessary for the foundation on which the block was laid to be truly horizontal and, secondly, that the base of the block when suspended should be in a horizontal plane. The first requirement was met by levelling work from within the diving bell. The second requirement was, however, more difficult to achieve. The blocks varied in weight from 140 tons to 360 tons and were not homogeneous, being composed of mixtures of large and small stones, gravel, sand, cement and water. Purser Griffith used wooden models of the blocks suspended by a fine thread to determine the centre of gravity or vertical axis of each block by trial and error. As the wood used was generally homogeneous, unlike the blocks, the method can only have been moderately accurate. Nevertheless, the block-laying was carried out very successfully and no real problems were encountered in maintaining the correct relationship between block and foundation.

LONGITUDINAL SECTION OF FLOATING SHEARS SHOWING ARRANGEMENT

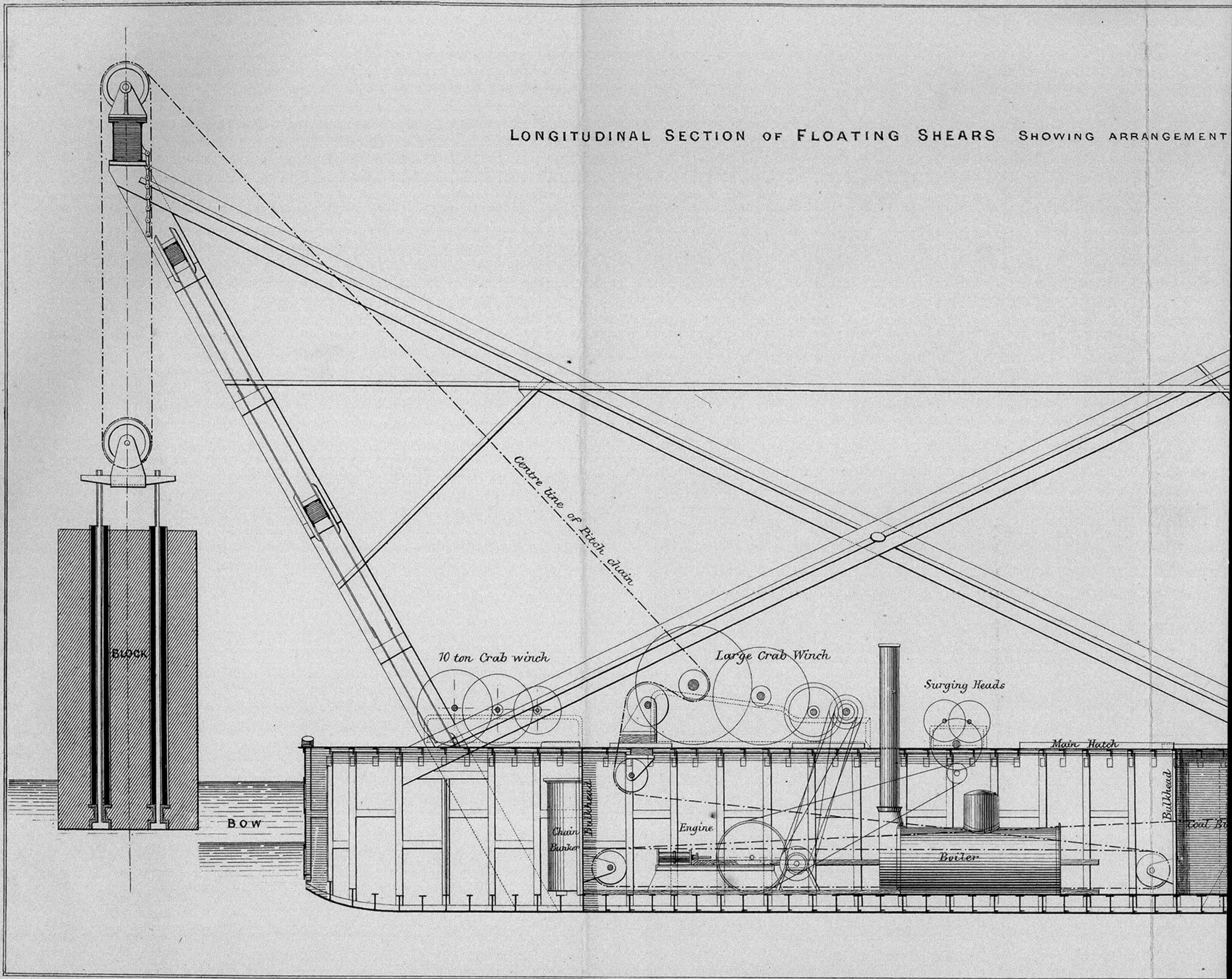
Centre line of Pitch chain
BLOCK
BOW
10 ton Crab winch
Large Crab Winch
Surging Heads
Main Hatch
Chain Bunker
Bulkhead
Engine
Boiler
Bulkhead
Coal B

Illustrating Mr. B. B. Stoney's Paper or

Plate I.

END ELEVATION OF FLOATING SHEARS.

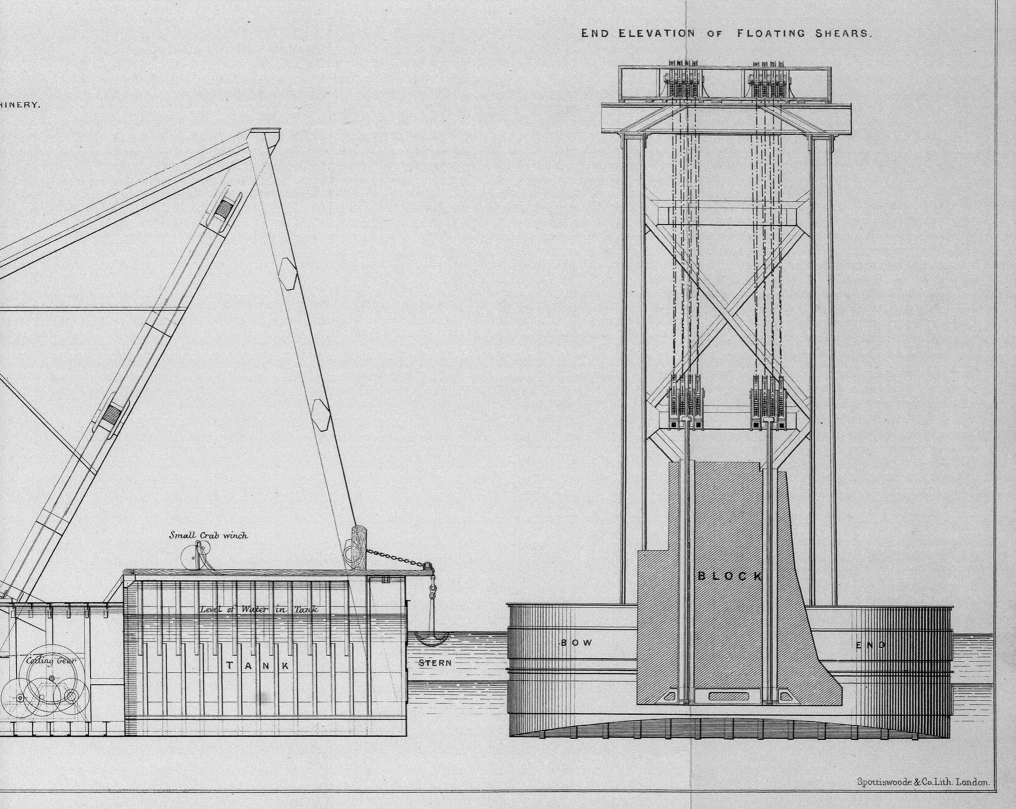

...HINERY.

Small Crab winch

Level of Water in Tank

TANK

Cycling Gear

STERN

BOW

BLOCK

END

Spottiswoode & Co. Lith. London.

...t Improvements in the Port of Dublin.

The opening of Alexandra Basin

During the early part of 1885, Stoney had been called upon to help in making the arrangements for the visit to the port of HRH Prince and Princess of Wales, in particular their visit to the North Quay Extension for the purpose of naming the recently completed basin. A temporary pavilion was erected on the West side of the Extension facing the Basin, in order that the royal couple could, in comfort and in the short time allotted, inspect the method of constructing the quay wall.

Stoney and the Harbour Master, William Carpenter, were pestered for tickets for the ceremony. There appears initially to have been a dearth of tickets available, and Stoney was moved on one occasion to write to the Secretary to the Board as follows: 'Dear Proud. Kindly send me down by messenger 300 to 400 red tickets... (they were originally blue, but the date of the ceremony was changed and the tickets were reprinted in a different colour to avoid confusion)...The enclosure will hold 1500 to 2000 people and many respectable people are asking for tickets and we have none. The place will look deserted if we don't issue lots of red tickets to respectable people — no time to close. Don't forget the CHAIRS. Yours in haste, B.B.Stoney.'

A letter to Proud dated 9th April, 1885 from a Jack Perrin, writing from the Custom House Docks Office, is worth quoting in full as an example of the extent to which 'respectable' members of the populace were prepared to humble themselves in order to procure tickets for such a royal occasion: 'My dear Mr Proud. Many thanks for the Ticket you kindly sent me for the "Alexandra Basin" Ceremony. You will understand that I am particularly anxious to bring my girl and sister... (the latter no doubt to act as chaperon)... — send me three more tickets and I will do as much for you some other time — Yours sincerely, Jack Perrin.'

As to the ceremony itself, the Irish Times reported: 'Shortly after their arrival (on the 11th April, 1885) the machinery sustaining the great concrete block was in motion, and the gigantic mass commenced to drop into its place in the water. Dr Bindon Stoney led their Royal Highnesses to the pavilion entrance and briefly explained to them the construction of the quay wall, after which the Princess, pulling a silken cord, broke the bottle of wine, and, amidst the cheers of the assembled multitude and a Royal Salute of 21 guns fired from the Pigeon House Fort, named the new dock "The Alexandra Basin".'

The report in the Illustrated London News of the 18th April recorded that the new Basin was 'christened by dashing a bottle of champagne against the end of the quay'. The engraving shows their Royal Highnesses accompanied by the unmistakable figure of Stoney — a proud moment indeed for Dublin Port's Chief Engineer. I like to think that his four year old only son was somewhere in the background watching the ceremony from the safety of his mother's skirts.

Princess of Wales naming the Alexandra Basin, April 1885

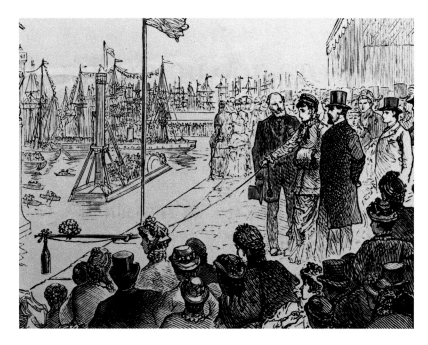

The Princess, pulling a silken cord, broke the bottle of wine, and, amidst the cheers of the assembled multitude and a Royal Salute of 21 guns fired from the Pigeon House Fort, named the new dock 'The Alexandra Basin'.

Other Dublin Port activities

Shipping movements

Despite depressed world trading conditions following the Crimean War, the tonnage of vessels using the port during the period 1860 to 1878 doubled. Having reached a peak of just over two million tons in the latter year, the average annual tonnage settled down to around 1.8 million for the remainder of the century.

The extensive harbour improvements effected by Stoney and his staff during the 1860's and 1870's undoubtedly contributed significantly to the considerable growth in the number of shipping arrivals and departures, with a consequent increased throughput of goods and prosperity for the Port.

The North Quay Extension afforded ample room for vessels and provided tidal-berthage accommodation of a depth then unknown in most harbours throughout the world. Large vessels plying the overseas trade were able to safely discharge their cargoes alongside the new berths and coasting steamers were able to sail at fixed times independent of the tidal conditions.

Construction work was now at a peak in the port and Stoney's fame was spreading. He had also won the heart of a lady! Following his marriage to Susannah Frances, daughter of John Francis Walker of Grangemore in Co. Dublin, Stoney began looking for somewhere larger to raise a family. In 1881, he moved with his wife and new-born son, George Bindon, into a substantial terraced house and mews at 14 Elgin Road, yet another address in what is now Dublin 4. Here he was to reside for the remainder of his life. The union was also to be blessed with three daughters, Priscilla Louisa Frances, Laura Kathleen, and a third child which sadly died shortly after birth. Shortly after he was married Bindon was honoured by the University of Dublin with an Honorary Doctorate of Laws and was also conferred with Fellowship of the Royal Society.

Other works

By the time that work on the North Wall Extension had ceased, Stoney had amassed a sizable fleet of marine construction and dredging vessels and equipment. On the dredging side, the Board owned three steam bucket dredgers, nine hopper barges, fourteen floats and a tug. The shears and bell floats, with their ancilliary crane, concrete, and other floats, constituted the main investment in heavy construction equipment. In addition, there was an assortment of steam and hand cranes, pumps, and a steam piling machine.

The North Wall Extension had taken Stoney and his Port & Docks workmen fourteen years to complete one of the most significant works in the development of the Port of Dublin. Just short of 5,000 feet of deep-water berthage was provided by the project and over £0.75 million was expended on harbour improvements during the first two decades of the new Board's existence. Such a sum may be regarded as a relatively minor investment when compared with expenditure on civil engineering projects across the Irish Sea during the same period, but was significant in terms of the funds available to support projects in Ireland. What was achieved for the money is indicative of the value of Stoney's original concept of quay wall construction using large masonry concrete blocks which proved to be more economical than the more traditional methods of the day.

Between 1875 and 1877, the floating shears was also used to transport and lay several large concrete blocks around the base of the Poolbeg Lighthouse, in order to protect the foundations from excessive wave action. The lighthouse had been transferred to the Board from the Irish Lights Commissioners in June 1876. Following this, two blocks were placed to form the foundations of a new lighthouse at the end of the North Bull Wall, the bed having been first prepared using the diving bell. On completion of the foundations, a four-storied iron tower lighthouse, reaching to a height of 58 feet above low water, was erected during the summer of 1878.

The celebrated politician, W. H. Gladstone, then between premierships, visited the port in October, 1877 and was given a demonstration of the block laying. Other visitors to the block-laying operations were members of the British Association for the Advancement of Science, meeting in Dublin in August, 1878, who were conveyed downriver on the 'Rose' to inspect the harbour improvement works.

Right:
Additional concrete blocks positioned around base of Poolbeg Lighthouse

Far right:
Cross sections of North Wall Quay, 1872

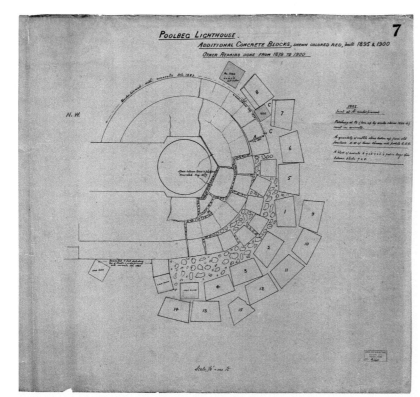

In August 1875, Stoney prepared estimates and details of a method of constructing a 50 foot diameter concrete base for the Daunt Rock off the Cork coast. He proposed to build it in a dry dock, float it out to the site, and sink it on to the bed rock, a procedure akin to the later floating caisson method of harbour construction.

Due to the pressing necessity having arisen to rebuild without delay a further portion of Sir John Rogerson's Quay, the Board resolved to discontinue further expenditure on the North Wall Extension as soon as the Pier Head of the Eastern Breakwater had been completed. So, in 1884, the North Wall Extension was left tailing off into a gravel slope and the skilled labour force was transferred from the North Wall to rebuild 800 feet of quay wall on the south side of the river extending west to Creighton Street at an estimated cost of £40,000.

From 1885 onwards, engineering work at the port was limited to the further deepening of the South Quays. By 1888, nearly 6,000 feet of shallow river quays had been reconstructed to substantially increase the number of deep-water berths, but tonnage of shipping had fallen to around 1.6 million. This was partly due to the change in the method of calculating the tonnage, but also to the general economic depression of the 1880's. Between 1889 and Stoney's retirement in 1898, no major works were undertaken (either reconstruction or new work) as the Board's borrowing powers became exhausted. Stoney was even asked to reduce expenditure on essential maintenance.

Stoney had proposed in 1883, and again in 1895, the removal of the then eastern breakwater and the building of an extension to Alexandra Basin and the North Wall. This was substantially the same as the scheme which was built in the late 1940's as Ocean Pier. His proposal was to construct a new angled breakwater in order to create an easier approach to the Basin, an idea which he had originally put forward as far back as 1862. As matters turned out, it was not until the 1930's that the then Port Engineer, Joseph Mallagh, completed the North Wall Extension using floating caissons, followed later by the completion of Ocean Pier.

Following cessation of the work on the North Wall Extension, the shears float was moored at the end of the extension and later served as a berth for tugs. The shears Float was actually classified as a vessel afloat, thus requiring a valid certificate of seaworthiness. Whilst forwarding it to the Ministry of Shipping in London, the certificate was lost on the S.S.Leinster when the vessel was torpedoed off the Kish Bank in October 1918. In the same month the shears float was sold to Hammond Lane Foundry and broken up for scrap. It seems strange that it was not offered for hire or sold to some other port authority to undertake similar work of quay wall construction, but the traditional method of working within a coffer dam was normally preferred, in spite of the proven savings in construction costs at Dublin.

Earlier, in 1903, the Board had been invited to contribute items for the United Kingdom exhibit at the International Exhibition (Louisiana Purchase Exposition) at St.Louis, which was scheduled to take place the following year. The Board sent models and drawings of the shears float and bell float and pontoon. The result was that Stoney was awarded the Grand Prize Diploma in Group 26 and a Commemorative Bronze Medal.

The lack of engineering activity in the port at the end of the nineteenth century can readily been appreciated from a study of the annual reports. Stoney's last Engineer's Report - that for the year 1897, contained nothing of note, apart from a statement of the amount of material dredged, and even that was only about one third of what it had been in the 1870's.

In 1898, as Stoney was retiring from his long association with Dublin Port, the first facilities for the storage of petroleum were in course of being established in the port for the Anglo American Oil Company and a new dawn was breaking over Dublin Port.

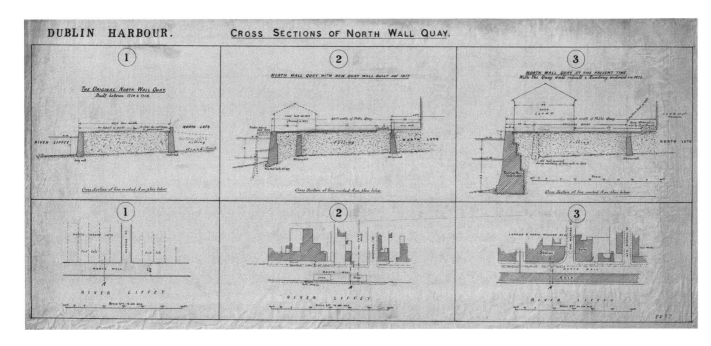

In 1898, as Stoney was retiring from his long association with Dublin Port, the first facilities for the storage of petroleum were in course of being established in the port for the Anglo American Oil Company and a new dawn was breaking over Dublin Port.

Dredging operations

The construction of deep-water berths in Dublin Port would have been pointless if the river channel had remained in a shallow state and had not been deepened. Prior to 1860, the average annual amount of material dredged from the harbour did not exceed 150,000 tons, largely representing the demand for ballast by the shipping using the port.

Following the establishment of the Dublin Port & Docks Board, the Harbour Improvement Committee estimated that, after completion of the various works contemplated, future annual dredging would exceed 700,000 tons. The dredging power available in 1869 was deemed inadequate to maintain a navigable channel, yet alone improve the situation. Tenders were therefore advertised for a powerful new steam dredger, three steam hopper barges, and six iron floats.

The new dredger arrived in the port towards the end of 1871 and, after having its buckets fitted, proceeded to undergo trials. The hopper barges did not arrive until the following year. Well over £500,000 was expended on new plant between 1869 and 1873 for preserving and improving the navigation of the river.

John Purser Griffith, who had joined Stoney's staff in 1871, in his paper to the Institution of Civil Engineers on the Improvement of the Bar of Dublin Harbour, alluded to the size of the dredging plant employed. He gave it as his opinion that it was probably unsurpassed in any port, noting however that dredging was essentially the application of sufficient mechanical power, whereas the improvement of the bar by artificial scour was 'essentially a triumph of civil engineering in its more restricted sense, forming a noble example of "directing the great sources of power in nature for the use and convenience of man" (a reference to the original Charter of the Institution of Civil Engineers).

Once the new dredging plant, had been acquired, an extensive programme of dredging was begun, priority being given initially to deepening the river opposite the new quay walls along Sir John Rogerson's Quay and the North Wall. Attention then turned to the longer term project of deepening and straightening the channel to provide access to the berths at all states of the tide for the class of shipping using the port, in particular the channel between Ringsend and the Pigeon House, and later to the Poolbeg Lighthouse at the port entrance. The Trawler Pond on the south side of the river opposite the North Quay Extension was also considerably extended by dredging.

The annual tonnage of dredged material, shown graphically in diagram on following page, indicates clearly the period of intense activity associated with the various quay reconstruction and new quay building projects resulting from the implementation of Stoney's recommendations to the Harbour Improvement Committee.

In the 1870's, dredged material was used to fill in between the two lines of blocks forming the North Quay Extension, but the work was frequently interrupted by the dredge floats being required to meet the sudden large demands for ballast by shipping. The peak of over one million tons dredged in 1876 was due largely to the completion of dredging in front of the new quay walls. This allowed the dredgers to work longer at straightening and deepening the channel east of Ringsend, where the work was more regular and less interrupted by constant shipping movements than was the case along the quays.

At the same time, the North Wall (subsequently named the Alexandra) Basin was being dredged out to depths varying from 14 feet to 24 feet below low water, the greater depth being alongside the new quay walls.

The bulk of the dredged material was taken out in large hopper barges, designed by Stoney, each of which carried 850 to 1000 tons of material, according to the state of the weather, to a distance of eight miles from Dublin, or about two miles beyond the Bailey Lighthouse off the Nose of Howth, and there deposited in deep water beyond the influence of tides within the bay. This method of disposing of the dredged material proved very economical and was a major factor in the success of the project to create a deep-water port for the city of Dublin. As the dredging proceeded further eastwards towards the harbour mouth, much of the deep dredging was executed in very hard ground, thus accounting to a large extent for the reduction in the annual tonnage of material recovered.

In October of 1880, Commander Langdon, R.N. was invited to carry out a survey of the river showing depths below the Dublin Harbour datum. Langdon was acting at the time as one of the Fishery Pier Commissioners, working out of the Custom House and commenced the harbour survey on completion of his duties for the Commission. The survey, which was subsequently published by the Admiralty, showed that considerable improvements had taken place in the river channel since the previous survey in 1856.

By 1881, it was clear that the dredging plant was rapidly wearing out, and a contract was placed with Messrs McIntyre & Co. of Paisley for the supply of a new steam dredger, and with Messrs Workman, Clark & Co. (Ltd.) of Belfast, to supply three hopper barges. These vessels added materially to the efficiency of the dredging department. Deepening and widening of the channel was chiefly concentrated on those locations where the sounding survey showed it to be necessary. A further survey of the river was carried out by Purser Griffith in 1889, which showed that the channel, although considerably improved, still required a large amount of dredging to bring it up to the standard set by Stoney.

Dredging could at times be a risky business, exposed as the crew were to the elements and forced, by the very nature of the task, to long periods of relative immobility in the midst of the busy shipping lanes. This is amply illustrated by referring to a serious incident that took place around 7 p.m. on the 22nd October, 1883. Steam dredger No. 4, whilst moored in the channel, was run into by the steam collier Annie about 350 feet SSW of the Flash Light on the North Bank below the Pigeon House. Immediately afterwards the unfortunate dredger was also hit by the P S Duke of Leinster, both of which sank in deep water.

A contract was placed with the Glasgow Salvage Co. to raise the dredger, and seven months after the sinking, it was delivered to the Board with serious damage to its hull, engines, boiler and machinery. The Board commenced a suit against the Annie for damages and judgement was subsequently entered in favour of the Board. Proceedings were taken against the Board by the owners of the Duke of Leinster for damage caused to their vessel and a cross case was entered by the Board against the said owners.

The Court of Admiralty decided that the collision occurred through default of the Board, but subsequently that decision was reviewed by the Court of Appeal, who decided that the damage arose from inevitable accident, and that neither party was to blame. A petition of appeal to the House of Lords was then lodged by the Dublin & Glasgow Steam Packet Co., owners of the Duke of Leinster, against the judgement, but the Lords upheld the decision of the Court of Appeal and awarded costs to the Board.

Damage was also often caused by steamers passing the dredgers at a high rate of knots. Rules had in fact been laid down by the Board in 1872, including an instruction to masters of vessels navigating in the river to stop their engines whilst passing any of the port vessels engaged in dredging or other works.

Arising from a complaint from a steamer captain of abuse from a member of the crew of one the dredgers, Stoney was forced to extract an explanation from the Supervisor of Floats, John Nolan, as to the circumstances under which the incident had occurred. Nolan's reply sums up the feelings of the dredger crews and, in particular one James Brady, and is quoted 'in extensio'. The incident also serves to illustrate how immune we have become to hearing expressions of dubious language which would have shocked our Victorian ancestors!

'I have to inform you in reference to Capt. Boxer's complaint (that) the crew of No. 1 Hopper told me that the Alexandra passed them nearly at full speed on Christmas Eve while alongside No. 3 Steam Dredger, making such a large swell in the river that it snapped one of the float's cast-iron timber heads. James Brady one of her crew cried out 'go slow you bugger' being much annoyed at the unnecessary trouble the Alexandra gave them. The men of the hoppers complain that lately they never slacken speed when passing the steam dredgers, often causing their spring ropes to break and on that occasion the damage might have been much more serious as the hopper had (on board) 800 tons of mud and (there was) a great fresh in the river at the time. I asked Brady if he knew the meaning of the word bugger and (he) said he did not nor mean any offence to anyone on board the Alexandra.

As dredging requirements declined in the late 1880's, the Board began to dispose of some of the hopper floats, a number of which were sold to the Tilbury Lighterage Co. of London. The steam dredgers were generally laid up and recommissioned whenever a large dredging job required to be carried out. In 1895 a contract was entered into with the Dutch firm of J. & K.Smit for the machinery for a large capacity suction dredger. The dredger began work the following February, chiefly tackling the deposits of fine sand which drifted into the channel from the North and South banks. However, the new dredger was not able to work to full capacity owing to the shortage of hopper floats, sold off earlier in an effort to reduce expenditure. In addition to this, the suction dredger was damaged by an incoming steamer in October, 1897, and laid up, bucket dredger No.5 being substituted. It was clear, however, that the suction dredger was superior to the bucket dredgers, particularly when raising mud and sand.

Lebby in America is generally credited with being the first to use suction dredging in Charleston Harbour in 1855, the Dutch and French making progress with its development in Europe in the 1870's. By the 1890's, suction dredgers were gaining in popularity, Liverpool introducing them in 1893, followed, two years later by Stoney at Dublin. Griffith was able to take full advantage of suction dredging when he took over from Stoney in 1898, thereby considerably accelerating the dredging programme.

Damage was also often caused by steamers passing the dredgers at a high rate of knots. Rules had in fact been laid down by the Board in 1872, including an instruction to masters of vessels navigating in the river to stop their engines whilst passing any of the port vessels engaged in dredging or other works.

Dredging Record: Port of Dublin 1870–1900

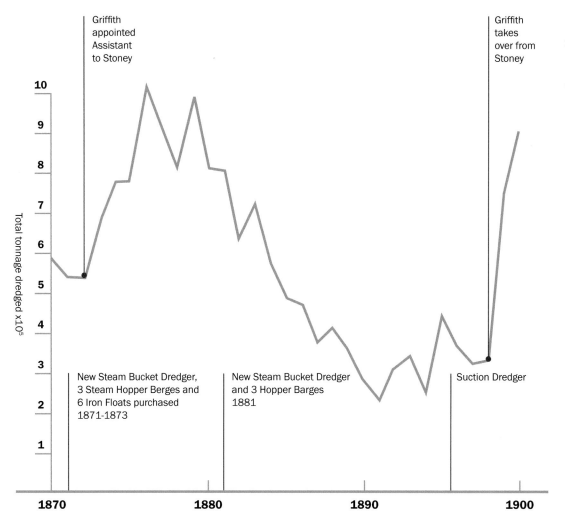

Griffith appointed Assistant to Stoney

Griffith takes over from Stoney

Total tonnage dredged x10⁵

New Steam Bucket Dredger, 3 Steam Hopper Berges and 6 Iron Floats purchased 1871-1873

New Steam Bucket Dredger and 3 Hopper Barges 1881

Suction Dredger

1870 1880 1890 1900

Engineering personnel

As we have seen, Stoney was appointed Assistant Engineer to the Ballast Board in 1856, at a salary of £250 per annum. By 1866, it had risen to £1000 per annum, comparing favourably with the salary of contemporary port and harbour engineers. As activity in the port began to increase, Stoney received assistance in the form of Isaac G. Mann. Mann graduated in engineering from TCD in 1862, being appointed Assistant Engineer in 1865 on a salary scale of £200 to £400 per annum. Mann's duties were listed as accounts, stores and like duties, in other words more of a clerical job, although he was given engineering work to look after, such as the Burgh Quay Reconstruction Project. In 1875, the Board proposed abolishing the position of Assistant Engineer, probably for financial reasons, but Mann pleaded for retention of the position. It was, however, abolished in June, 1881, and Mann was forced to retire having been made redundant. The Board added thirteen years to his years of service and he was granted a pension of £240. Mann was not replaced, mainly due to the fact that engineering work in the port had begun to decline. He later became Engineer to Rosslare Harbour, before retiring to live in England, where he died in 1917.

The appointment in 1871, at the commencement of the construction of the North Wall Extension, of John (later Sir John) Purser Griffith, began a partnership which was to last until Stoney's retirement. Griffith's initial salary was £150 per annum, reaching £800 prior to succeeding Stoney in 1898. Griffith's duties were (as listed in 1880) to ' assist in making surveys, plans, specifications and estimates; to set out, measure and inspect works; assist in office correspondence, preparation of reports and management of the Department, and to represent the Engineer in his absence.'

By contrast, Stoney's duties were not specified, but his office hours were given as 10 a.m. to 4 p.m., a seemingly leisurely lifestyle and more than enough time to read the Times of London, given in the Dictionary of National Biography as Stoney's sole leisure activity! It would appear that Stoney was being somewhat reticent in not mentioning his many other extramural pursuits. Stoney and Griffith shared the responsibility for engineering work in the port for a period of 27 years (1871 — 1898), assisted by a number of young engineers, who were from time to time taken on for short periods as articled pupils.

In 1872, the Board increased Stoney's salary to £1500, this representing the normal maximum of the scale. The recommendation of the Harbour Improvement Committee is interesting and important as it explains in large measure why Stoney did not apply his practical knowledge and skill as a consultant to other harbour projects to the extent that one would have expected of such a national expert.

The report, dated 23 September, 1872, reads as follows: 'The Committee having taken into consideration the length of service of Mr Stoney as Engineer of the Port, and the eminent ability and success, with which he has planned and executed works of great importance for the accommodation of the increasing trade, and as Mr Stoney has hitherto given, and undertakes to continue to give, his professional services exclusively to the port, the Committee unanimously recommends that his salary be advanced to £1500 a year from the present time. 'The recommendation was duly adopted by the Board at a special meeting held on 3 October. By comparison, the salary of the next highest paid official, the Secretary to the Board, Nicholas Proud, was only £1,000.

Stoney had a long association with the Institution of Civil Engineers of Ireland, acting as its Hon. Secretary between the years 1862 and 1870, and becoming President for the Session 1870-71. He was also a member of the Council of the Institution of Civil Engineers and travelled as often as he could to meetings of that Institution in London. His strong links with shipping led him to seek membership of the Institution of Naval Architects, later becoming a Fellow. Stoney was elected a Member of the British Association in 1857 when only 29 years of age, and was also an active contributing member of the Royal Irish Academy throughout his life.

Plans and elevations of North Bull Lighthouse, January 1874

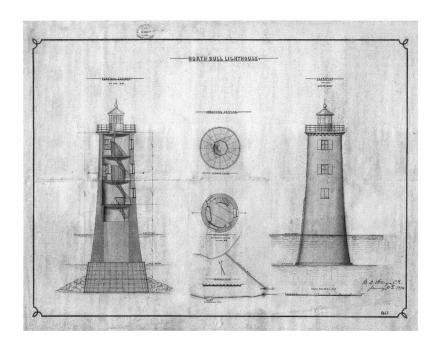

As we have seen, Stoney was appointed Assistant Engineer to the Ballast Board in 1856, at a salary of £250 per annum. By 1866, it had risen to £1000 per annum, comparing favourably with the salary of contemporary port and harbour engineers.

Bridging the Liffey

Grattan (Essex) Bridge

An Act passed in 1811 extended the Ballast Board's responsibility for maintenance to 'all the bridges now over the said Anna Liffey or which hereafter may be built or erected within the said limits over the same'. The 1870's saw a flurry of bridge building activity as the trade of the city moved further downstream and, as Chief Engineer to the port, Stoney was called upon to undertake the design of a number of bridge widening and reconstruction projects up-river from the port.

The first of these projects was the rebuilding of Essex Bridge, named after Arthur Capel, Earl of Essex, Lord Lieutenant 1672-77, originally erected in 1676 by Sir Humphrey Jervis, and rebuilt in 1753-55 by George Semple. Semple was of the opinion that it would 'last as long as the little adjacent mountain called Sugar-Loaf Hill.'

In October, 1865, a number of leading citizens petitioned the Corporation to do something about Essex Bridge, as it was too narrow and had very steep approaches. The City Engineer, Parke Neville, having advised the Corporation that the bridge was the responsibility of the Ballast Board, Stoney was asked by the Board to prepare plans and estimates for lowering the bridge. The first of two schemes which he submitted involved the removal of the existing arches and the erection of a new cast-iron girder superstructure on Semple's piers and abutments.

Stoney remarked at the time that 'although the architectural effect may be open to criticism, as is generally the case when an old bridge is modified, yet an excellent bridge may be constructed for far less than a new one.' The alternative design, which was the one eventually proceeded with, involved substituting a series of flatter segmental or elliptical arches for the lofty crowns of the existing semi-circular arches and carrying the footpaths beyond the face of the arches on cantilevered iron girders.

The cost of implementing the first design was estimated at £9,142 and the alternative design at £12,205 plus in each case £1,798 for the provision of a temporary timber pedestrian bridge. The Corporation were asked to decide which design should be adopted. Apart from the fact that the Ballast Board did not have the money to rebuild Essex Bridge, other more momentous happenings were imminent. The days of the Ballast Board were numbered and, in 1867 the newly constituted Dublin Port & Docks Board assumed responsibility for the bridges over the river Liffey upstream as far as and including Victoria (now Rory O'More) Bridge near Kingsbridge (now Heuston) Station.

It had been decided that the reconstruction of Essex Bridge should be carried out in advance of that of Carlisle Bridge, the plan being that Essex Bridge would carry diverted traffic and in November, 1870, the Corporation further advised the new Board that the improvements would have to be in accord with and in furtherance of the Main Drainage of the City and that the plans and specifications would need to be altered and modified accordingly. It was agreed that Stoney and Parke Neville should thrash out the details between them.

The second of the original designs was adopted with some modifications by the Corporation, but with the financial proviso that they would only pay the Board instalments of £4000 per annum on the total cost of around £14000. The Board's Law Agent advised that the Corporation could not do this, stating that the Corporation had a simple duty to perform under the Act 17 Vic., Cap 22, either to sanction the estimate or to reject it. If sanctioned, they were bound to insert the full estimate in the schedule of applications to the Grand Jury and when fiated (sanctioned) the Collector General was bound to levy the amount and lodge it in 'The Quay Wall and Bridge Tax Account'. In spite of this, however, the Schedule for 1870 (No. 70) showed, £4,000 as the first of four instalments.

By August 1871, the cost of the rebuilding had risen to £17,256 and there was opposition to the project from some of the ratepayers, particularly those who had property within the city boundary, but whose principal residence lay outside.

The Schedule of Presentments for 1871 included the revised figure, but proposed that it now be spread over twenty years! Naturally, the Board were not amused and returned to the courts to fight for the total cost to be paid over as a single sum. Stoney advised the Law Agent that the job would take about two years to complete and a compromise was reached whereby the Corporation would pay the Board one-third of the total sum in 1873 and the balance the following year on the certificate of the Chief Engineer.

As the abutments of the bridge had to be rebuilt to accommodate the main drainage ducts, a sum of £6,200 was included in the total, it was agreed that the portion of the costs resulting from the provision for the main drainage be met by the Main Drainage Committee, the remainder i.e. anything to do with the bridge, being the subject of a presentment. The revised presentment was fiated by the Grand Jury in November, 1872, and Stoney was given the go-ahead to prepare revised plans and specifications and to go to tender.

Essex Bridge following rebuilding

By August 1871, the cost of the rebuilding had risen to £17,256 and there was opposition to the project from some of the ratepayers, particularly those who had property within the city boundary, but whose principal residence lay outside.

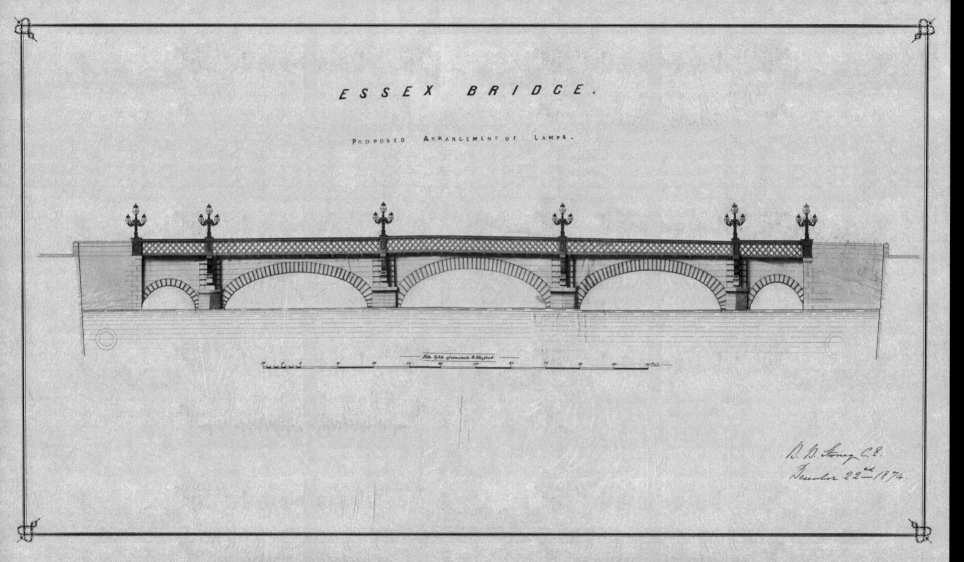

ESSEX BRIDGE.

PROPOSED ARRANGEMENT OF LAMPS.

Scale 1/4th of an inch to the foot.

B. B. Stoney C.E.
December 22nd 1874.

Stoney worked closely with Parke Neville during the carrying out of the contract by William J.Doherty, of the South Quay Works, with whom the Board entered a contract in March, 1873. The unsuccessful tenderers were Hammond of Drogheda and Collen Bros of Dublin. The tender prices were extremely close, that from Doherty actually being the highest. Doherty was of course well known to the Board for his excellent work on the reconstruction of the South Quays and thus had the edge over his rivals.

When the work of rebuilding the bridge finally got underway, there was a petition from traders on both sides of the river to construct a temporary timber footbridge opposite Swift's Row to open up a route to Dame Street. This particular location was selected as the quays were wider and the river narrower at that point. There had also been a petition for the temporary bridge to be sited so as to link Essex Quay and Upper Ormond Quay. In the event both groups got their way. The bridge at Swift's Row consisted of eleven spans, the central or navigation opening being 30 feet wide. The wooden bridge was popular, but obstructed navigation and was removed at the end of the project, much to the relief of Guinness's who operated barges up and down the river conveying the magical black liquid for which Dublin remains famous!

The plans, prepared by Stoney, called for the arches of the new bridge to be elliptical instead of semi-circular. Semple, when rebuilding the bridge in 1753-5 had used semi-circular arches but was not, it seems, sufficiently courageous to adopt the ellipsis, leaving it to Telford to initiate its use in large-span arches. Semple's bridge had been modelled after Labelye's Westminster Bridge in London, and it was generally accepted that, had Semple provided a flatter profile, and hence a level roadway, his bridge would have lasted much longer. As it was, traffic dictated that the bridge be substantially rebuilt by Stoney.

As soon as the temporary bridge was opened, the work of taking down the old bridge was begun. In order to avoid disturbing the parts of the piers and abutments which were to be retained, centring was erected under each arch and well wedged up to them. Cutting-out of the key courses of the five arches was begun simultaneously from both faces of the bridge, working towards the axis, about three feet of the key course being left uncut until as much of the arch sheeting as possible had been racked down. The result was that, on finally cutting out the keystones, a comparatively small weight had to be carried by the centres, and no undue lateral pressure was exerted on the piers. Most of the arch stones of the old bridge were sufficiently large and

sound to permit of being redressed and used again in the new arches. Extra stone was quarried in Dalkey in south county Dublin and shipped to the site from Bulloch Harbour near Dalkey.

The ironwork for the cantilevered footpaths was supplied and erected by Courtney, Stephens & Bailey of Dublin. They were highly criticised by the writer in the Irish Builder of October, 1874, who felt that (the footpaths) 'are being supported upon the most primitive looking and certainly the clumsiest attempts at corbelling ever beheld, and which appear to have been designed (by Stoney) after the model of the working carpenter's antiquated ogee bracket.'

What was considered to be a substantial and solidly built structure now stood in place of Semple's artistic work, but it was felt that the footpaths, cantilevered on wrought-iron girders, 'altogether destroy what might have been at the same cost a highly creditable work'. The writer went on to remark that 'our only regret is that it (Semple's Essex Bridge) is not replaced by a structure at least as ornamental as he (Semple) produced. No doubt the third (Stoney's) bridge is well and solidly built, but there is something more which a city like Dublin demands, and that is for its rising generations it shall not appear to be retrograding in its architectural features.'

In order to accommodate the main drainage, the quays were widened near the bridge, so destroying the continuity of line. Stoney disapproved of the widening on the river frontage and felt that instead the building line should have been moved back in view of the fact that most of the properties were rather old and decrepit.

In a letter dated 14th March, 1876, Stoney, referring to the lamp supports, wrote that 'The seahorses have been copied from a piece of stucco work, apparently a fountain, supported on three horses, not two as in the lamp design, and I think the effect of their flappers, which somewhat resemble the fore feet of a seal, would have a weak effect, especially in the view which would be presented to persons walking along the footpaths'.

After the rebuilding and widening, the bridge was renamed Grattan Bridge after Henry Grattan (1746-20). Maurice Craig has described it as 'the ugliest bridge in Dublin' and one has to admit that the addition of the cantilevered footpaths, although of historical engineering interest, do not say much for Stoney's aesthetic judgement, but then the Port & Docks Board were always hard pressed to raise the funds required for these capital intensive projects and Stoney would have been very conscious of the need to propose economical solutions to the problems set before him.

The plans, prepared by Stoney, called for the arches of the new bridge to be elliptical instead of semi-circular. Semple, when rebuilding the bridge in 1753-5 had used semi-circular arches but was not, it seems, sufficiently courageous to adopt the ellipsis, leaving it to Telford to initiate its use in large-span arches.

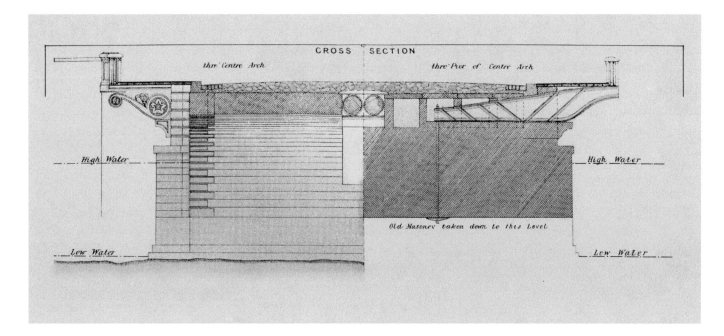

The increased commerce and development of the city generally in the early 1860's soon made it obvious that Carlisle Bridge (built 1791) was too narrow and awkwardly hump-backed, but it was not until 1880 that the citizens of Dublin were able to benefit from the rebuilding of this late eighteenth century structure. Seventeen years of debate, competition and politicising were to ensue before so much as a stone was laid. Much of the delay was occasioned by the protracted negotiations between Dublin Corporation and the Dublin Port & Docks Board.

In 1860, a traffic survey found that between 9am and 7pm on an average working day, some 10,000 vehicles crossed Carlisle Bridge between a quarter and a third of these making turning movements on to the bridge from the quays. The extension of building, and the increase in population had taken place in an easterly direction and this, combined with the rapid development of commerce, the establishment of a railway system centred on Dublin, and the general economic improvement in the country, had shown the inadequacy of the bridge. The traffic from the 230 foot-wide Sackville Street and the quays on the north side of the river, together with the two thoroughfares and quays on the south side, combined to pour across the 40 foot width of the bridge.

The Corporation, urged on by the leading promoter of the project, Alderman Reynolds, set up a Committee in 1861 to report on the practicability and probable expense of rebuilding Carlisle Bridge. There were, even at that stage, some objections to the idea of an iron bridge, presumably on account of the narrowness of previous iron bridges. The Carlisle Bridge Committee recommended that the new bridge should be as level as possible, be the same width as Sackville Street, have stone abutments with iron carriageway and superstructure, and that it should make provision 'to do honour to illustrious men' by way of statuary and other suitable embellishments.

A conceptual design for an iron bridge of single span was received in May, 1862 from Richard Turner and George Page. However, in 1864, it was decided to hold a competition to find the best design, and some 40 designs were received and considered, some serious, some trivial and easily discounted. The judging Committee, consisted of Sir Richard Griffith, Col. J.G. McKerlie, and Sir Thomas Larcom (later to be replaced on the committee by Professor Samuel Downing). They selected three designs, in order of merit.

The winning design was that which had been submitted earlier by Richard Turner of Dublin (the creator of the Palm Houses at the Botanic Gardens at Dublin, Belfast and London) and George Gordon Page (son of

Thomas Page, the builder of Westminster Bridge, London). The design was for a single arch of 140 foot span in cast and wrought iron with a rise of 10 feet 6 inches. It was to be constructed of cast iron from abutments to within 25 feet of crown of arch, the 50 foot centre piece being of wrought iron. The abutments were to be of stone. The principle had already been carried out with great success at Westminster Bridge in London.

Turner and Page's design envisaged as embellishments, the City of Dublin arms and motto on the spandrels, Irish Harp and Shamrocks to fill up spaces. Equestrian figures — Queen and Late Prince Consort (died 1861) at Sackville Street end, Wellington and Gough at the other end, the centre of the bridge carrying the coat of arms of Viceroy Carlisle.

Doubts, however, were expressed as to the structural soundness of the Turner and Page design as conveyed by their drawings. The arch appeared to be too flat, the abutments needing to be either further out into the river, thus impeding navigation, or else the ends of the girders must be under water at high tide, leading to corrosion problems. There were still plenty of advocates for a bridge composed of two or three masonry arches, an iron bridge being regarded by many as out-of-place in a city centre sporting some fine examples of the architects' art. The runner-up design was from the firm of Lanyon, Lynn and Lanyon, Architects, and was for two masonry arch spans. Placed third was the design of May and Pole. Another entry, that of J.Halton, entitled 'In Memoriam', although 'a work of beauty and artistic merit' was rejected as the instructions of the competition had not been entirely complied with. It was, however, an intriguing design which would certainly have provided a centre-piece for modern Dublin!

Arranging finance for the project proved difficult and Reynolds, an Alderman of the City made several attempts to get the Westminster Parliament to vote the necessary £30,000 to £40,000 without success. And so things languished until the new Dublin Port & Docks Board tried again in 1868, maintaining that a large amount of funds had been drawn from Ireland since the Act of Union (1800) and expended in London 'instead of being appropriated to works of usefulness or ornament in this country.' A deputation, consisting of three members from each of the Corporation, the Port & Docks Board and the Dublin Chamber of Commerce, went to London to petition the government for funding for the new bridge. They also wrote to Gladstone, who referred them to the Chancellor for the Exchequer, who simply said 'no'.

COMPETITION DESIGN FOR PROPOSED NEW CARLISLE BRIDGE—Submitted by Messrs. Turner and Page, C.E's.

COMPETITION DESIGN FOR PROPOSED NEW CARLISLE BRIDGE—Motto, "In Memoriam."

Opposite page:
Cross section of Essex Bridge illustrating footpaths, cantilevered on wrought-iron lattice girders

Left:
Competition designs for proposed new Carlisle Bridge — Motto, "In Memoriam"

Both illustrations published in the Irish Builder & Engineer, 1868

Dublin Port Chief Engineers
Bindon Blood Stoney (1828-1909)

The Irish Builder of 1868 concluded that 'whatever design may be selected for the new bridge, we presume the works will be carried out under the supervision of the able engineer to the Board, B.B.Stoney,Esq., whose skill and scientific knowledge are well known to the citizens of Dublin'.

By May, 1870, Turner, despairing of ever building his iron bridge in the heart of Dublin, transferred responsibility for the project to his son Thomas and the plans were once again submitted to the Board for their inspection. Richard Turner wrote that he would be happy to have Thomas,' who is a Civil Engineer', explain the plans to the Board.

Later the same month, the Corporation asked that Stoney and Parke Neville, examine the structure of the existing bridge and report upon the stability or otherwise of the foundations and abutments. In July, Stoney reported that the masonry of the abutments, piers and arches was in good order, and no apprehension need be felt about the stability of the bridge. Parke Neville concurred with Stoney's assessment.

The Board then sought the opinion of their Law Agent, Joseph Hone of 5 Foster Place, as to the exact powers given it under the Act 17 Vic., Cap 22. Hone replied that the Board had absolute power to judge when it was necessary to repair or rebuild the bridges under its jurisdiction, including Carlisle Bridge. The Board had the power to transmit estimates, decide on plans, contract for and carry out works 'when, and as soon as, money was lodged to their credit', such money 'to be levied by the Municipal Corporation as directed in the Act.' The Board would not, however, be entitled to build a 'new bridge', unless the existing bridge was dangerous and even then 'if such estimate was transmitted by the Board and inserted by the municipal Council in the Schedule of Estimates before the Grand Jury, that 'such estimate could be traversed and with success by any rate payer.' Different interpretations as to what constituted a new bridge or a rebuilt bridge, and hence responsibility for the cost of undertaking the project, was the principal cause of the inordinate delays in making a start on solving the problem of the worsening traffic congestion at the heart of the city.

The Carlisle Bridge Committee meanwhile had asked the Board to meet it, afterwards resolving to recommend the plan for a stone bridge prepared by Lanyon, Lynn and Lanyon at a cost of £44,000. The design envisaged two spans with a central river pier. On the 25th August, Stoney was asked to have a provisional estimate ready for forwarding to the Corporation before 1st September (the date specified in the Act for the receipt of estimates for works to be included in the estimates for any year).

The plans, prepared by Stoney, called for the arches of the new bridge to be elliptical instead of semi-circular. Semple, when rebuilding the bridge in 1753-5 had used semi-circular arches but was not, it seems, sufficiently courageous to adopt the ellipsis, leaving it to Telford to initiate its use in large-span arches.

Stoney naturally protested that he could not possibly produce a reliable estimate in such a short time, but hazarded a guess by saying that he thought it would cost £80,000 or more. At this stage, the Board put the project 'on the back burner' and informed the Corporation accordingly. However, the design controversy continued unabated.

In August 1870, Gordon Page wrote to the Board challenging the estimate from Lanyon, and saying that he would find a contractor who would build the Page & Turner iron bridge for £30,000. The matter was referred to Stoney for comment. The following December, Page & Turner again wrote to the Board reminding it that their design had won first place in the competition, and submitting general plans to add to the perspective drawings already with the Board. Again the plans went straight to Stoney.

At the end of March, 1871, Stoney submitted two designs in stone, he himself being in favour of stone where it could be adopted,' especially for a metropolitan structure, where permanence and durability may be expected.' He estimated the cost of his preferred design at £61,500 and selected granite as the most suitable stone. Stoney felt that the bridge should have two or more arches, but if it was decided to proceed with an iron bridge, then the design of Turner & Page would do well with some modifications. However, he did not believe an iron bridge would have the lasting qualities of stone. He was also of the opinion that the cost of constructing a single central pier and the temporary works involved would offset any savings in arches.

In May of the same year, Page announced that he was preparing a cheaper design for an iron bridge and Richard Turner was still pushing to have his son build the winning design. At the end of July, Page & Turner duly submitted a detailed estimate for an iron bridge at a cost of £30,000. On hearing this, Lanyon, Lynn and Lanyon reminded the Board of their design for a stone bridge, and so the controversy continued.

Stoney reported that, in his opinion, the modified design submitted by Page & Turner was materially different from that which had been submitted in the competition. The new design envisaged placing the pedestals and parapets inside the frontage line of Sackville Street and leaving an open space in the centre of the roadway, thus creating in effect two bridges. The arches had been raised and the rise at the crown increased by one foot, thus making the bridge as high as the existing structure. Stoney found that many parts had been changed to reduce the cost to below that of a stone bridge. He estimated the cost of the new iron bridge at around £66,000 as against a relatively maintenance-free and cheaper stone bridge.

Four years were to elapse before the Board met with the Corporation to revive the project. In August 1875, the Board recommended Turners' revised iron bridge design at a cost of £34,472, although Parke Neville considered it much of an underestimate. The Board left it until the 31st August to ask Stoney to examine Turner's plans and estimates, and prepare a report for the Board to meet the 1st September deadline! (shades of 1870). Needless to say, all that Stoney could do was protest at the lack of notice and agree with Neville that the cost of an iron bridge had been grossly underestimated. In any case, the proposed iron cylinders projecting out into the tideway would have looked hideous in the location.

The Board requested Stoney to prepare a proper estimate and give a considered opinion as to the engineering merits of Turner's design and, in addition, to prepare a plan and estimates for a three-arch masonry bridge, the width of Sackville Street, and utilising the existing structure as far as possible. This is the first reference to Stoney designing the bridge as actually built.

Top:
Work in progress in 1879 on Carlisle Bridge

Far left:
Carlisle Bridge prior to rebuilding

Left:
Iron caisson for pier extension

Stoney's estimate for the new bridge was £74,000. There was also talk of another bridge East of Carlisle Bridge, the most favoured location being Beresford Place. However, Stoney was not in favour of an opening or swivel bridge as he thought it would be too disruptive to land traffic and considered that the extra cost of operating it, capitalised at say £10,000 to £12,000 would go a long way to providing berths elsewhere in the Port, for example at East Wall, to replace those along the river quays, such as Eden Quay. This would also, he felt, avoid eventual public pressure to change the opening bridge to a fixed structure as port traffic moved further downriver.

The estimate of £74,000 for rebuilding Carlisle Bridge included provision for main drainage syphons as proposed by the consultant to the Corporation, Joseph Bazalgette. In the event, these were eventually located in a tunnel under the river further downstream, so the estimate was reduced to £64,000, later to be increased again to £68,000.

In 1876, the subject of improved and increased bridge accommodation was again brought forward by the Corporation for consideration by the Board, accompanied by a signed memorial from leading Dublin merchants and traders requesting the erection of an opening bridge eastwards of Carlisle Bridge, and the rebuilding of the latter to the same width as Sackville Street. The Board agreed to promote a Bill in Parliament and the Dublin Port & Docks Board (Bridges) Act, 1876, received Royal Assent on the 27th June, 1876, enabling the Board to carry out the two projects.

So, on 26th July, Stoney was able to place before the Board 'an alternative design for Carlisle Bridge with elliptical in place of segmental arches' giving 'an enlarged waterway and less of a flooded appearance during winter high tides.' The following day, the Board approved the plan and sent it to the Corporation for approval and to the Grand Jury for fiating. After considerable negotiation, the Lords Commissioners of Her Majesty's Treasury agreed to advance an amount, not exceeding £130,000, and at the rate of 4% interest, repayable over 25 years, to finance the building of the two bridges.

An outline of the specification for widening and rebuilding Carlisle Bridge appeared in the Irish Builder for May, 1877, when the tenders for it and for the new-swing bridge were advertised (The full specifications had already appeared within the pages of The Engineer). It was proposed to lower and alter the existing approaches, to build a new superstructure to correspond with the width of Sackville Street and to divide the traffic across the bridges by a central footway, on which were to be placed three ornamental five-light lamps 'in the highest style of Parisian art.' The footways were to be of best Limmer asphalt (the Limmer Asphalt Co. had been established in 1871) laid in two thicknesses, with granite curbings. The entire work was to be completed within two and a half years from the date of contract under penalty of £30 per week for every week beyond that time. The specification provided that at no time during the progress of the works should the thoroughfares along the quays, across the bridge, or along or across the approaches, be blocked.

The contractor for both the Carlisle Bridge and Swing Bridge projects was William J.Doherty, who submitted the lowest tender for £110,269 16s Id. Apart from Grattan Bridge, Doherty had completed a considerable amount of quay wall rebuilding for the Board between 1869 and 1877, and Stoney had been very impressed by the standard of workmanship achieved by Doherty's men on the Sir John Rogerson's Quay and other river contracts.

Doherty began work in May, 1877, the early months being devoted to erecting the temporary staging and the construction of the coffer-dams at both sites. At Carlisle Bridge, Doherty used single balk dams, the design of which had been suggested by Stoney as far back as 1870, as it was essential that the waterway be encroached on as little as possible. The construction of these dams, which were specified in the contract, was assisted by what was termed group or panel pile driving, i.e. each pile consisted of two or three whole balks of timber fastened together by dowels and strapped across with wrought-iron dogs. Driving piles in groups reduced the number of joints to be caulked to make the dam water-tight. Doherty had experienced problems at the south pier of the Beresford Place site with the more traditional double-row coffer dam and he elected to use the single balk dams for the north and central piers. The results were dramatically successful and the method of construction was subsequently reported by Purser-Griffith in a paper to the Institution of Civil Engineers of Ireland in 1881.

Large iron caissons, manufactured by the Skerne Ironworks in Darlington, were used to form the extensions to the existing piers to support the masonry arches carrying the widened Carlisle Bridge. The caissons were framed together and riveted up, in a strong platform, 13 feet above low-water, and about 12 feet above high-water mark. When ready for lowering, a strong staging, composed of sixteen vertical 12-inch timbers, was erected, and a platform built over the caisson. From this platform the caisson was first lifted off the bottom platform by means of eight two-inch diameter screw jacks and then, the bottom platform being removed, lowered down 10 feet at a time to its position on the bedrock. The overlying stratum of mud was then cleared away by diving and dredging operations, and the caissons filled with concrete. Once the extended piers were completed, construction of the superstructure of the bridge could begin.

The exceptionally severe weather experienced in Dublin towards the end of 1878 however, caused a disruption in the supply of stone and progress slowed. The arches of the side additions were completed by May, 1879 and the thoroughfares over these, together with the temporary foot-bridges, were then opened to the public. The superstructure of the old bridge was then removed and the new abutments, piers and arches belonging to the central portion of the new bridge, together with the greater part of the eastern parapet were completed.

One of the final tasks was left to the sculptor, Harrison, who faithfully copied Edward Smyths' original carved heads of Neptune and Anna Livia. The original heads now adorn the facade of the former Tropical Fruit Co.'s Building on Sir John Rogerson's Quay. However, Maurice Craig called Harrison's reproductions 'mediocre.'

When completed the Board named it Carlisle Bridge and a handsome red marble tablet on the bridge actually carries the name Carlisle Bridge. The City fathers subsequently covered it with a bronze-green plate which, as Little has remarked in an article in the Dublin Historical Record, is the one which 'greets the passer-by today who little dreams that the brilliance of Dan envelops the dullness of the Earl'.

The Corporation renamed the bridge O'Connell Bridge as they were in the course of erecting a memorial to the patriot at the southern end of Sackville Street. However, there had been a plea from a writer in the Irish Builder to name either of the two new bridges after James Gandon, whose Custom House is located nearby, pointing out that to the shame of Dublin, Gandon 'sleeps in the grave with no slab or line to mark the spot, save the tombstone of his bosom friend, Francis Grose, the antiquary, the architect and antiquary being interred in the one grave in the village churchyard of Drumcondra.' The contractor, Doherty, also had connections with Drumcondra, living at the time in Clonturk House, to the garden of which he had the balustrading of the old bridge removed and where it can still be seen to this day. The rebuilt O'Connell Bridge was finally opened to the public on 6th August, 1880.

Beresford Swing Bridge:
Pier and Mechanical
details, published in
The Engineer, 1879

Dublin Port Chief Engineers
Bindon Blood Stoney (1828-1909)

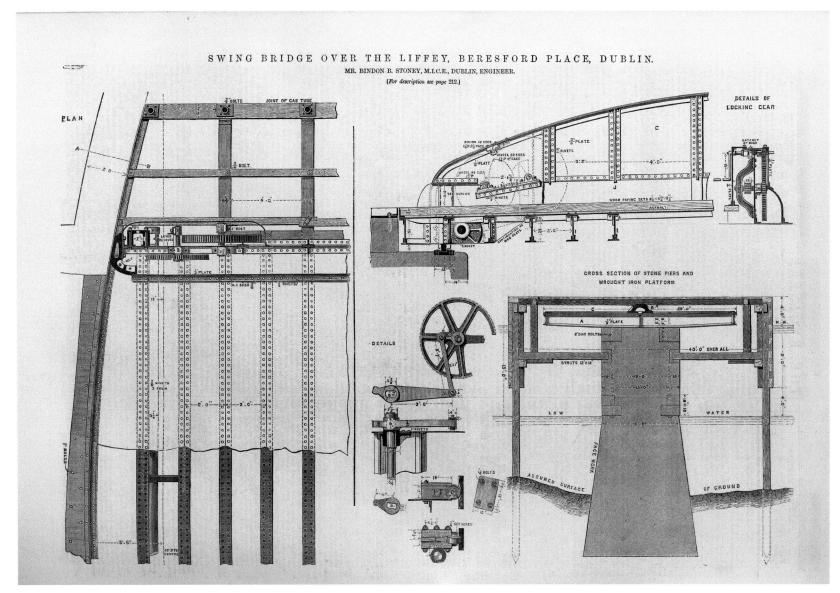

SWING BRIDGE OVER THE LIFFEY, BERESFORD PLACE, DUBLIN.

MR. BINDON B. STONEY, M.I.C.E., DUBLIN, ENGINEER.

(For description see page 212.)

Beresford Swing Bridge

The construction of the Beresford Swing Bridge was a more straightforward project, entailing as it did the construction of two approach spans of 37 feet each and a central swing span of 127 feet, giving two 40 foot openings for navigation. The roadway was 18 feet 6 inches wide, with two footpaths of 5 feet 6 inches each, the gradient being about 1 in 28. The general contractor was again W.J. Doherty, the ironwork and the machinery being supplied by the Skerne Ironworks in Darlington, the suppliers of the caissons for Carlisle Bridge. Nabholz of the Skerne Ironworks designed the steam engine which provided the motive power for opening the bridge, although it could also be opened manually.

Stoney designed the swing span as a pair of parabolic wrought-iron web girders connected by 60 cross girders under the roadway plates, on which asphalt and wood paving sets were laid. The girders were carried on a wrought-iron platform mounted on top of a central pier, the engine house and other ancilliary equipment being mounted on a timber pier on the downstream side of the bridge, tied into the masonry pier and supported in addition from the river bed. Provision was made in the scheme for the subsequent removal of the swing span and its replacement by a single central stone arch to link the two smaller side arches.

The Irish Builder writer was of the opinion that the Beresford Swing Bridge should have been sited further downstream in order to provide a handier connection between the Westland Row and Amiens Street railway termini. This was before the Liffey Viaduct and approaches were built, which effectively prevented the swing bridge from ever opening again and forcing its eventual replacement. Architecturally minded citizens were also concerned that the swing bridge would visually detract from Gandon's masterpiece, the Custom House.

The first test of the machinery for operating the opening span was made on 7th November, 1878, in the presence of Stoney, his assistant Purser-Griffith, Nabholz of the Skerne Ironworks, Galwey, an articled engineer under Stoney, and Doherty, the contractor. All went well and it was found that the swing span could be opened in one minute and closed again in a similar time.

The swing bridge connected Beresford Place on the north side of the river to Tara Street on the south side and was opened on 26th August, 1879, but not used for regular traffic until the 9th of the following month. There was no special opening ceremony, but several members of the Corporation were present, together with officials connected with the shipping interests, and some members of other public bodies.

BUTT BRIDGE

— PLAN OF OPENING BRIDGE —

BUILT IN 1879

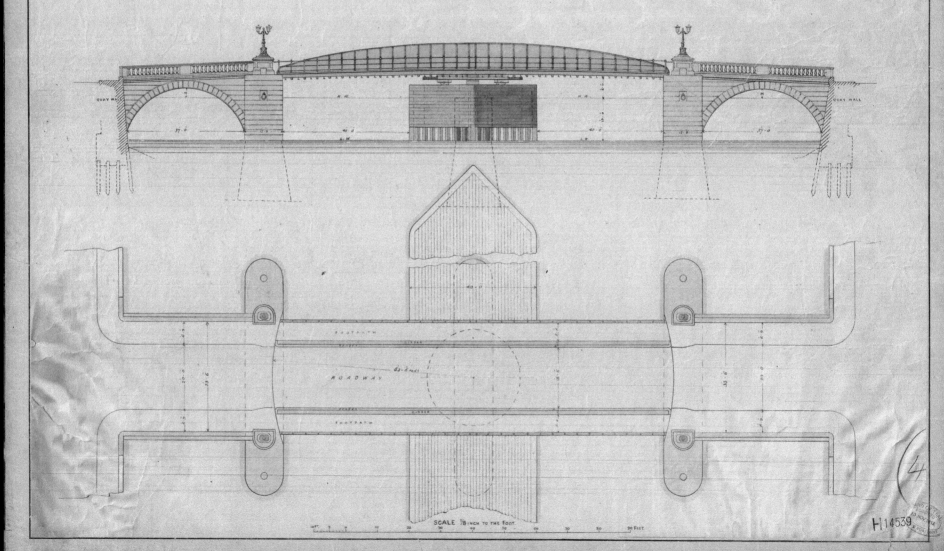

QUAY WALL

QUAY WALL

FOOTPATH

ROADWAY

FOOTPATH

SCALE ⅛ INCH TO THE FOOT.

Dublin Port Chief Engineers
Bindon Blood Stoney (1828-1909)

Opposite page:
Elevation and plan of Beresford Swing Bridge as built in 1879

Top:
Beresford Swing Bridge, looking towards the Custom House

Right:
Beresford Swing Bridge before demolition to make way for Butt Bridge

Openings of Beresford Swing Bridge 1879–1888

Year	Up River	Down River	Time Open (Hours/Minutes)
1879	59	61	9.27
1880	168	156	17.44
1881	124	130	18.42
1882	42	45	8.38
1883	48	47	9.09
1884	75	77	19.48 (incl. repairs)
1885	58	59	10.12
1886	52	53	9.08
1887	34	33	4.43
1888	13	14	2.18
Totals	**673**	**675**	**109.50**

The average opening time for each vessel was approx. 5 minutes.

54

Dublin Port Chief Engineers
Bindon Blood Stoney (1828-1909)

**Beresford Swing Bridge:
Superstructure details,
published in The Engineer,
1879**

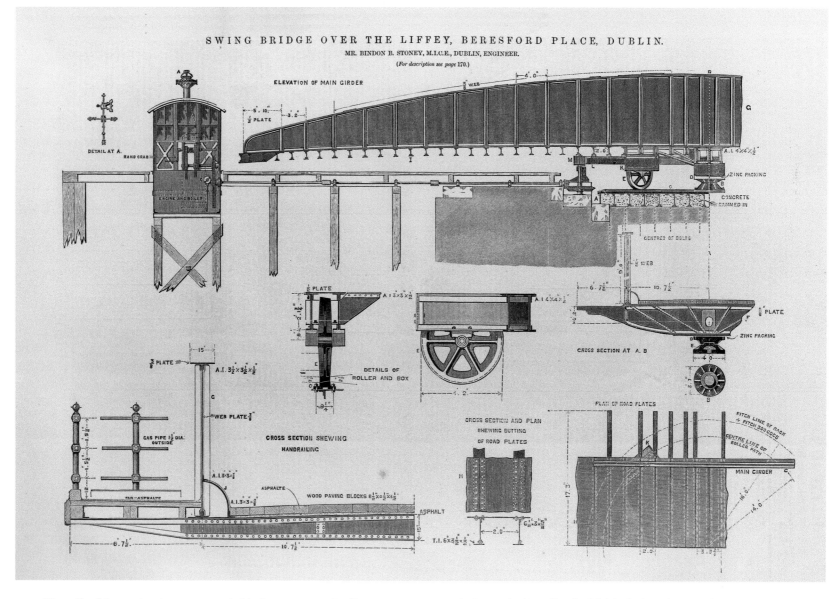

The wife of the contractor, accompanied by her son, were the first to drive across the bridge, followed by another vehicle carrying a soldier and some other men — then came the rush of the anxious crowd and the event was over. Purser-Griffith deputised at the opening for Stoney, who it seems was away on his honeymoon, having recently entered the state of matrimony at the mature age of 51!

The importance of the bridge to Dublin commercial life may be judged from a record of traffic movements during the period Monday, 27th October, to Saturday, 8th November, 1879 (exclusive of Sunday), between the hours of 9 a.m. and 7 p.m. Quoting from the Annual Report of the Dublin Port & Docks Board for 1879: 'The vehicular traffic, which embraces carriages with and without fares, and drays laden and unladen, shows that 18,147 Vehicles passed over the bridge from north to south, and 19,982 from south to north within the period, or an average of 3,177 vehicles daily.' In addition, it was reported that during the same period, a total of 2,232 cattle, 384 equestrians and 75,693 pedestrians had passed over the bridge.

As Stoney had predicted with his design, the Beresford Swing Bridge was operational for barely eight years before the construction by the Dublin, Wicklow, and Wexford Railway Company (City of Dublin Junction Railways) of the Liffey Viaduct effectively blocked the progress of all shipping upriver, apart from the Guinness barges and other light craft, and on 13th December, 1888, the bridge was closed for the last time. The Board received £7,000 in compensation for the loss of revenue from the Eden and Burgh Quay berthage.

With further increases in the volume of road traffic, the narrow and steep roadway soon became a constant source of congestion and, as early as 1896, proposals were made to the Board for the widening of the bridge. It was not until 1932, however, that the central swing span was removed and replaced with a single reinforced concrete arch spanning between the two original side arches.

At the end of 1881, for his work in designing and supervising the rebuilding of Essex and Carlisle bridges and the design and construction of the Beresford Swing Bridge, Stoney received a special payment of £1,000 guineas. This represented, it was reckoned, a sum equal to only about one fifth of the professional fees that the Board would have had to pay out if their own Chief Engineer had not undertaken the work. This was the Board's way of recognising Stoney's valuable contribution to the improvement of communications in the city and the port area generally.

Stoney's research, publications and consultancy

Dublin Port Chief Engineers
Bindon Blood Stoney (1828-1909)

PLATE II.

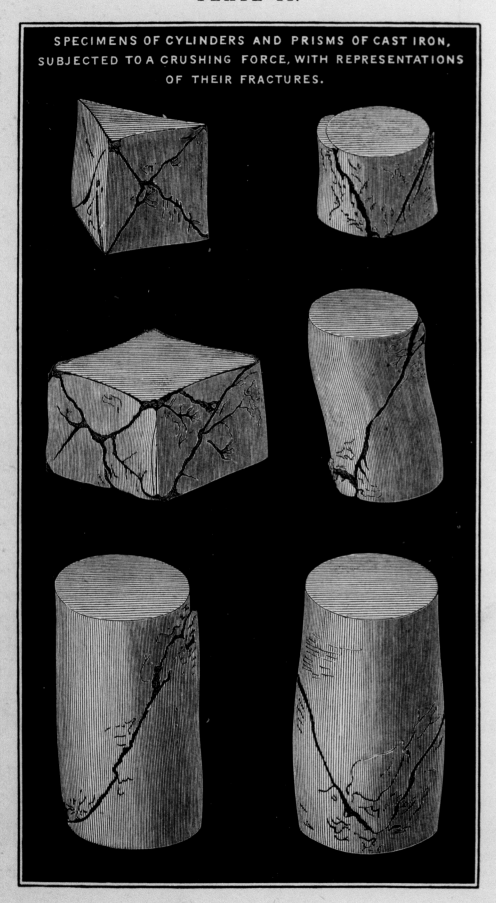

SPECIMENS OF CYLINDERS AND PRISMS OF CAST IRON, SUBJECTED TO A CRUSHING FORCE, WITH REPRESENTATIONS OF THEIR FRACTURES.

Stresses and strains in girders

As a member of a number of professional societies, Stoney, during his lifetime, contributed papers on a variety of engineering topics. His major contribution, however, was undoubtedly his treatise on Theory of Strains in Girders & Similar Structures, first published in 1866. The reviewer of the first edition of 1866 considered that the author 'has well employed his leisure time in its production.' In the preface to Volume 1 of the work, Stoney informs his readers that 'he wrote it at various times, during such brief intervals of leisure as the author could spare from his professional duties.'

The contents of the book were the result of experience combined with theory and, as such, filled an important gap in the engineering literature of the time. It was in effect a handbook on the theory of strains (stresses in modern terminology) and the strength of materials. As such, it gave practical methods for calculating the strains which occurred in girders and similar structures of the period. The theory of transverse strain had not been treated adequately by contemporary writers, their researches being confined to strains in plain girders, or to a few more elementary forms of trussing.

Stoney stressed that a thorough acquaintance with the theory of strains and the strength and other properties of materials formed the basis of all sound engineering practice. He noted that 'when this is wanting even natural constructive talent of a high order is frequently at fault and the result is, either excess and consequent waste of material, or, what is still more disastrous, weakness in parts where strength is essential!'

He rightly felt that the time was past when practical experience formed the sole qualification for high engineering success and it is worth quoting at length a description of the essential difference, as he saw it, between an engineer and a craftsman:

'The usual resource of the merely practical man is precedent, but the true way of benefitting by the experience of others is not by blindly following their practice, but by avoiding their errors as well as extending and improving what time and experience have proved successful. If one were asked what is the difference between an engineer and a mere craftsman, he would well reply, that one merely executes mechanically the designs of others, or copies something which has been done before without introducing any new application of scientific principles, while the other moulds matter into new forms suited for the special object to be attained; and though experience and practical knowledge are essential for this, he lets his experience be guided and aided by theoretic knowledge, so as to arrange and proportion the various parts to the exact duty they are intended to fulfil. The well-educated engineer should combine the qualifications of the practical man and of the physicist, and the more he blends these together, making each mould and soften what the other would seem to dictate if allowed to act alone, the more will his works be successful and attain the exact object for which they are designed. The engineer should be a physicist, who, in place of confining his operations to the laboratory or the study, exerts his energies in a wider field in developing the industrial resources of nature, and compelling mere matter to become subservient to the wants and comforts and civilization of the human race.' The application of sound engineering and scientific principles and a willingness to utilise new materials and develop new methods is nowhere more evident than in Stoney's creative work at the North Wall Extension and the Alexandra Basin.

The calculation of the strength of structures had largely been based on the physical investigations of Eaton Hodgkinson and others in England. The 'Report of the Commissioners appointed to Inquire into the Application of Iron to Railway Structures', published in 1849, was another source of information. It was generally accepted that 'every material is more or less ductile'. Stoney queried whether this was true of materials already stretched by applied strain. He followed Navier's Resume des Lecons donnees a l'Ecole des Ponts et Chausees in assuming that the coefficient (modulus) of elasticity is the same for compression as for extension (tension). In his table of Coefficients of Elasticity for various materials, Stoney quotes Tredgold, Hodgkinson, Young (for steel), Barlow, Trickett (an Australian) and Clark.

Later in the book, Stoney dealt with flanged girders with braced or thin continuous webs. The knowledge of strains in vertical webs was at the time still very imperfect and he went on to develop his ideas about diagonal strains in continuous web and lattice girders. Later we find an explanation of the value of curved flanges (as used later in the Swing Bridge at Dublin).

In all his writings he drew heavily on his experience when Assistant' to James Barton on the construction of the Boyne Viaduct. The diagrams in Stoney's book were engraved on wood by Oldham and printed white lines on a black background, i.e. reverse printing, a relative novelty at the time, and were highly effective.

His two-volume treatise (later editions were combined into a single volume) ran to several editions and became a standard reference work for designers. The reviewer of the 1873 edition felt that there was a great deficiency of information amongst architects, builders and their workmen in Ireland in regard to the strength and properties of building materials. In the case of stone, if it was from a long-worked and well-known quarry, it was assumed to be alright. The writer advocated that before any building stone from a new quarry be used, its strength should be tested by experiment. Although Stoney quoted in his work the opinion and result of the experiments of other well-known professional men on the strength and properties of building stones, he agreed with the writer that the strength of stone should be tested by actual experiment. The reviewer wished that the book contained more experimental results of tests on Irish building materials as used in public buildings. He also alluded to complaints about the quality of Irish bricks, which he described as 'full of rubbish and unsuitable clay.' By the time of the 1886 edition, it is evident from tables that Stoney had carried out experiments to determine the moduli of rupture of locally occurring materials, e.g. granites and limestones from the greater Dublin area and beyond.

Stoney was particularly interested in the properties of concrete and found that the crushing strength of Portland Cement Concrete, which had been compressed during placement, was considerably greater than that which had not been compressed. In his own practice, Stoney stated that he always had the concrete carefully rammed, and 'when it forms the matrix for large rubble stone, the concrete is compressed between the stones with iron tampers having T-shaped ends about 5 in. long. This permits it to be mixed stiff, with but little water, and, thus solidly rammed, the stones will generally break sooner than the concrete in which they are embedded', indicating a strong bond between cement and aggregate.

Opposite page:
The Fracture of Materials in Stoney B.B., *'Theory of Strains in Girders and Similar Structures'* 1868)

The contents of the book were the result of experience combined with theory and, as such, filled an important gap in the engineering literature of the time. It was in effect a handbook on the theory of strains *(stresses in modern terminology)* and the strength of materials.

In June, 1859, Stoney read a paper to the Royal Irish Academy 'On the application of some new formulae to the calculation of strains in braced and lattice girders'. The paper contained a modification and extension of the principles of bracing previously investigated by Professor W.B.Blood of University College Galway and Professor R.H. Bow. Stoney developed formulae for expressing the maximum strains in various classes of flanged girder and advocated the use of angle sections rather than flat plates for the struts in lattice girders in order to resist flexure at right-angles to the plane of the web.

Stoney, who was elected to membership of the Royal Irish Academy in June 1857, a year after his brother George Johnstone, presented two further papers to the Academy in 1862. The first of these 'On the strength of long pillars' appears to have contributed little to the understanding of the problems of buckling of pillars under load. Stoney's paper followed contributions from Professor Humphrey Lloyd and Sir William Rowan Hamilton, distinguished fellow contributors by any standard, and leading Irish scientists of his day.

In June, 1862, in a paper to the Royal Irish Academy entitled 'The relative deflection of lattice and plate girders', Stoney outlined the chief distinction between lattice and plate girders. The distinction lay in the formation of the web or vertical portion which connected the top and bottom flanges. In the former the web was formed of bars, intersecting each other at various angles, according to the design, but generally arranged so as to form a series of isosceles triangles, like lattice work. In the latter the web was one continuous sheet formed of plates riveted together. An example of the former was the original Boyne Viaduct, a smaller example still existing in the form of the Obelisk Bridge further up the River Boyne at the site of the famous Battle of the Boyne. The Britannia and Conway Tubular bridges are examples of the latter. When the flanges are horizontal, all the strains which are not horizontal in direction pass through the web, and are transmitted by it to the abutments or piers on which the girder rests.

In lattice girders, the directions of the strains were determined by that of the lattice bars, whereas in plate girders, it was not known what direction the strains took, although it was appreciated that there must be diagonal strain. Much ignorance prevailed on the subject and prejudice rather than reason often carried the day when the two systems came into conflict. One of the fallacies was that a lattice girder deflected more than a plate girder 'of equal strength'. The continuous plate web was, it was argued, capable of sustaining strains in every possible direction, and was therefore stiffer than a number of lattice bars with open spaces between them. This appeared plausible to many engineers at the time and was accepted without much investigation.

Although experience was gradually removing the prejudice against the use of lattice girders, Stoney decided that it was time to see how far theory and experience agreed. He prepared carefully constructed deflection diagrams at a highly exaggerated scale to show firstly, that the method of constructing the web had hardly any influence on the shape of the deflection curve, provided that the unit strains in the flanges remained unaltered, and secondly, that two girders of equal length and depth, one a lattice, the other a plate girder, having the same strains per square inch transmitted through their flanges, will deflect to the same extent.

Apparatus for testing strength of rivetted plates. Trans. R.I.A. — Science, Vol XXV, 1874

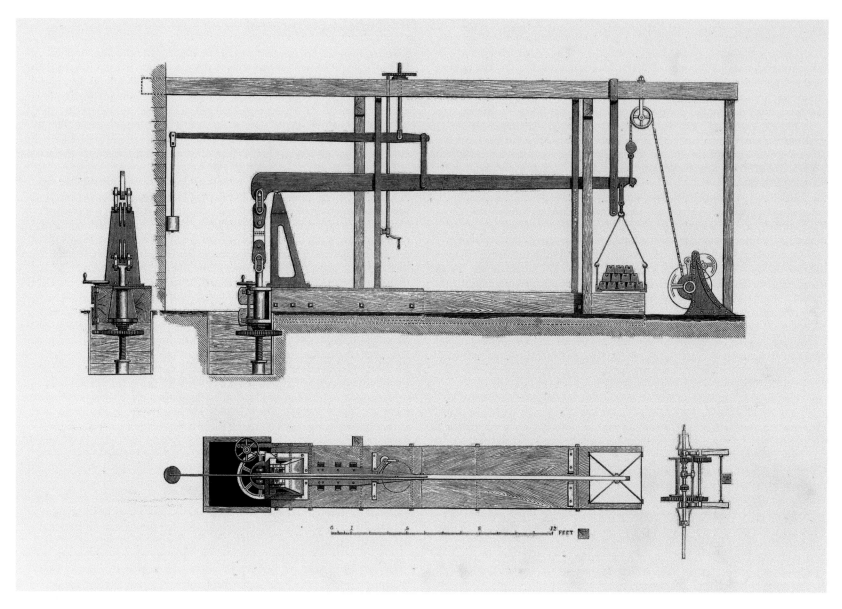

He proceeded to develop an expression for the deflection at the centre of a span in terms of the length of the girder, its depth, and the difference in length of the flanges after deflection, which proved useful to bridge designers.

'The Strength of Single-riveted Lap Joints' was the subject of a paper delivered by Stoney at the Royal Irish Academy meeting in June 1874. He had carried out an extensive series of tests using a lever testing machine which he had designed and had built in Dublin Port. The main lever of this machine was of wrought iron, with steel knife edges at the bearings; the lower arm of the lever being 20 feet, and the shorter arm one foot in length. Thus a weight of one cwt, or its fractional parts, in the scale hanging from the end of the longer arm produced a tension of one ton and its corresponding fractional parts in the specimen under test, which connected the shorter arm of the lever with a powerful adjusting screw secured to the base of the machine. The weight of the main lever was balanced by means of a small lever placed above and connected with its centre of gravity, so that the main lever floated and avoided the necessity of taking the weight of the lever into consideration when calculating strains.

Stoney investigated various arrangements of rivets in an attempt to observe the manner in which jointed plates failed and to determine the ratio of the breaking strength of single riveted lap-jointed plates to that of a solid plate. The plates used were 3/8" thick boiler plates and the rivets 3/4" in diameter, the riveting being carried out by hand. Hitherto, it had been customary, following the experimental work of Sir William Fairbairn, to assume the strength of single-riveted lap jointed plates to be 56% of that of a solid plate. Stoney found from his experiments that the figure was nearer 48% if holes were drilled, and only 44% in cases where the rivet holes were punched.

Over ten years later, in 1885, Stoney contributed an extensive paper to the Institution of Civil Engineers of Ireland on the subject of the strength and proportions of riveted joints in iron plating. He presented much new data from his own experiments, combined with a compilation of the experimental results of a number of the leading names in the profession. The paper dealt with the difference in shearing strength of rivets in drilled or punched holes, differences as a result of the method of riveting, including hand, machine, steam and hydraulic, and resulting from the design of the joint itself. The then President of the Institution, John Aspinall, was moved to carry out his own experiments at the Inchicore Railway Works in Dublin as he somewhat doubted Stoney's results, which gave a greater shearing strength to rivets in punched holes than to those in drilled holes. In the event, Aspinall drew no conclusions from his experiments and could find no fault with Stoney's claims.

Work on telescopes

In a paper to the Institution of Civil Engineers on the Construction of Floating Beacons, which Stoney presented in 1861, details were given of an improved type of beacon, which he called a Keel Buoy. The sides were extended below the bottom, so as to form a circular keel, which encompassed a large body of water. Thus such a buoy, six feet in diameter, with a keel of 18 inches, contained within the latter a body of water exceeding a ton in weight, or a mass of water of nearly the same weight as the buoy. Equal pressure was exerted above and below the centre of mooring, thus imparting great stability to the beacon and freedom from abrupt motions in most sea states.

Stoney came in for some criticism from the members present, who felt that he was not presenting anything new. Vignoles went so far as to 'deprecate the introduction of papers of a purely theoretical character, not descriptive of works actually constructed.' Stoney, in a written reply, rebutted this attack by pointing out that no fewer than seventeen of these Keel Buoys had been constructed, for Trinity House, the Ballast Board in Dublin, for Waterford Harbour, and even for the Russian Government. He also repeated his assertion that the Keel Buoy was more than just a modification of the earlier cone-bottomed type designed by a Mr Herbert in the 1850's. The President, Bidder, however, did not feel that it constituted more than a slight modification and, in any case, was not likely to perform the way Stoney hoped, so that was that. Perhaps this was a case of the London members of the engineering profession doubting that any new ideas could possibly emanate from engineers in Ireland. Whatever the reason for the frosty reception in 1862, they were in the years to come to recognise Stoney's undoubted expertise and originality in the field of harbour engineering.

In 1874, Stoney received the highest honour bestowed by the Institution of Civil Engineers of London for a paper by a member. The Telford Medal and Premium were awarded to Stoney for his paper 'On the Construction of Harbour and Marine Works with Artificial Blocks of Large Size." The contents of this paper have been dealt with in Chapter Four.

Consultancies

In 1872 Stoney began corresponding with the 4th Earl of Rosse regarding the rebuilding and remounting of the 36" Reflecting Telescope. He began by examining the various loadings which the equatorial axis would have to bear following modifications to the telescope. The letters are very detailed and include sketches of the various arrangements. There was little new in the suggested forms of mounting, but Stoney used his extensive structural engineering knowledge to offer solutions to the specific problems encountered during the rebuilding of the telescope and was largely responsible for the design. He suggested to the Earl that George Strype of Grendon's in Drogheda be retained as mechanical engineering consultant for the project. Strype later resigned his position with Grendon's, but continued to be involved with the telescope project. During the month of August, 1872, we find Stoney writing from 2 Grosvenor Terrace, Bray, where he was giving advice on the harbour and sea defences and no doubt taking the air at this popular Victorian seaside resort.

Part of the project at Parsonstown (Birr) involved the construction of facilities for the astronomical observers. Stoney proposed a circular tramway, with a travelling stage, erected on a carriage, up and down which the observer's cage moved vertically, the stage being capable also of moving longitudinally on the carriage. The adoption of this arrangement resulted in the eyepiece not moving on the surface of a sphere, but this was of lesser importance than the facility of observing. Stoney had seen a model at Exeter of Sir Howard Grubb's method of mounting and felt that there was merit in adopting a plan which had already been carried out successfully. He had also considered other methods, such as that by Lassell. Stoney also kept the Earl straight on contractural matters, advising him as to what was the norm in conditions of contract and setting down specifications for the work to be carried out.

The Earl took a keen interest in a range of scientific applications and was responsible for the first known proposal for the armour plating of warships and wrote a memoir on the subject for the Admiralty at the time of the Crimean War. Like Robert Mallet and others also discovered, the Admiralty largely ignored these bright ideas from members of the scientific community, choosing to allow their own officers to 'discover' the improvements in technology from within the government service.

In 1874, Stoney received the highest honour bestowed by the Institution of Civil Engineers of London for a paper by a member. The Telford Medal and Premium were awarded to Stoney for his paper *'On the Construction of Harbour and Marine Works with Artificial Blocks of Large Size'.*

Other papers

In return for a relatively large salary, Stoney had given the Board an undertaking that he would give his professional services full-time to the Board and concentrate his energies on creating, improving and maintaining the deep-water port. His role as a harbour engineering consultant was thus somewhat less than one might have expected, given his eminence in the field. Stoney was forced to ask permission for a few days 'leave of absence' each time that he wished to accept an invitation to give his advice on other projects.

Nevertheless, Stoney did act as a consulting engineer, reporting on or executing works for many harbours, particularly along the east coast of Ireland and to a lesser extent other coastlines. He had associations with all the major ports, with the exception of Limerick and Belfast and also advised on works in connection with railways, canals, reclamations and water power.

Between 1877 and his retirement in 1898, Stoney gave evidence to a number of Parliamentary Committees, examining the state of various public works, examples being Ballina Harbour and the Manchester Ship Canal, both in 1884. In the case of Arklow, Stoney travelled to Edinburgh to consult Thomas Stevenson, then 'an old and delicate man', and they submitted a joint report on the proposed harbour developments.

An example of the Board's reluctance to involve their Chief Engineer in too much outside work is evidenced by a Board minute in relation to proposed work at the People's Park in Blackrock near Dublin. The Board agreed that, as it was close to the city, he (Stoney) could act as consulting engineer, but not superintend the works.

The Irish Builder of July 1st 1875 published verbatim extracts from a consultant's report which had been prepared by Stoney in the matter of suggested improvements to the Port and Harbour of Drogheda in county Louth, a place of which he had been well acquainted during his time as Assistant to James Barton on the building of the Boyne Viaduct.

The Boyne Commissioners and Drogheda Corporation were portrayed by the Irish Builder as making 'the same endless resolves and counter-resolves, and (receiving) reports and amended reports, lawyers' opinions and engineers' opinions, including their own engineer, whose report was rejected. Finally, they turned to Stoney, but his report on the works did not seem to impress the representatives of the town of Drogheda, some of whom considered that they were as wise as before, to which the writer in the Irish Builder commented that 'they seem to be as wise as ever they are likely to be, as wisdom does not appear indigenous to their nature.' Further scathing remarks were reserved for the Commissioners, who were advised to 'give up their chronic wind blasts and drifting schemes, and to set about doing something practicable with the means at their disposal.'

In June, 1867, Stoney was asked for his opinion on the development of waterpower in Ireland. It cannot have been a very deep study as he requested no more than two days leave and thought that perhaps only one would suffice! He was later to be involved in the design of sluices on the river Erne at Belleek which controlled the flow of water from Lough Erne in order to maintain the navigation.

His role as a harbour engineering consultant was somewhat less than one might have expected, given his eminence in the field. Stoney was forced to ask permission for a few days 'leave of absence' each time that he wished to accept an invitation to give his advice on other projects.

The eminent engineer

Stoney's contribution as Port Engineer

In order to form an opinion as to the importance of Stoney's work in the Port of Dublin, it is worth comparing his achievements with those of Jesse Hartley. Dock Surveyor to Liverpool Dock 'Trustees between 1824 and 1860. Hartley was appointed in 1824 at the then large salary of £1,000 and a generation before Stoney. During his 36 years at Liverpool, Hartley was responsible for the building of four miles of river frontage, 21 new docks and 12 graving docks, quite apart from the altering, deepening and repairing of the original dock system, plus numerous structures, in particular the Albert Dock warehouses, bridges, machinery, roads, and railways. As full-time Engineer to the Dock Trustees, he was responsible for all planning, design and maintenance, much of the construction being by direct labour. In addition, he was much sought after as a consultant for bridges, canal locks and by smaller port authorities.

Hartley worked almost exclusively with granite, having the assistance of a number of master masons to direct the work. Stoney, on the other hand, developed an original method of placing large blocks of masonry concrete for port construction, and promoted the large-scale use of cement as a binding agent. As has been recorded in earlier chapters, he had to work with a very small staff and an extremely limited budget. The only significant assistance that Stoney could call on throughout most of his years in Dublin Port was his Assistant, John Purser Griffith.

It can be judged therefore that, although Stoney's achievements at Dublin were very different and on a smaller scale from those of Hartley, they were certainly accepted by the engineering community as being a valuable and significant contribution to the development of methods of harbour construction. Under Stoney's directions, half the former shipping quays along the Liffey were reconstructed and converted to deep-water quays, and several thousand feet of new quay walls were built using 350-ton blocks. In addition, a number of hopper barges, designed by Stoney in 1865, were at the time of unprecedented 1000-ton capacity.

On his retirement from the service of the Dublin Port & Docks Board in 1898, the staff and workmen of the Engineering Department spoke of their appreciation of all Stoney had achieved for Dublin. 'The Port of Dublin', they said,' must ever remain a monument of your genius and engineering skill', and again, 'The great strength and durability of the works attests to the soundness of his ideas and his positive genius for initiative in his profession.'

Shortly after the completion of the North Wall Extension Project, Stoney was the recipient of an Honorary Degree of Doctor of Laws (LL.D.) from the University of Dublin (Trinity College) at the Summer Commencements held on 30th June, 1881.

Dublin Port 1898

1 Grattan Bridge
2 Liffey Bridge
3 O'Connell Bridge
4 Beresford Swing Bridge
5 Inner Dock

6 George's Dock
7 North Quays
8 South Quays
9 Pigeon House Harbour
10 Poolbeg Lighthouse

11 North Bull Lighthouse
12 Crossberth
13 North Wall Extension
14 No.1 Graving Dock
15 Retaining Wall

16 Alexandra Road
17 Alexandra Basin

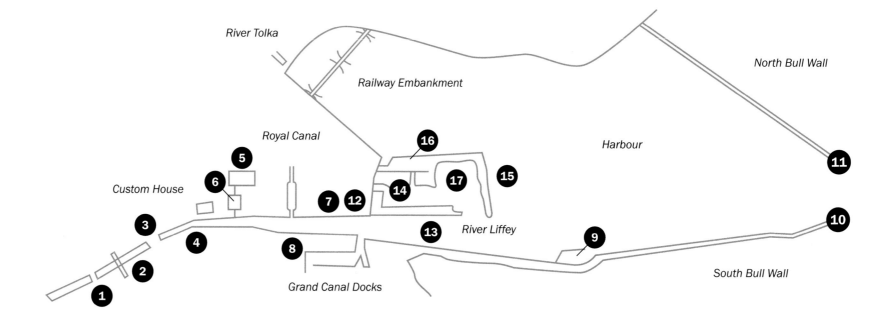

Stoney the thinker

The range of Stoney's mental activity was not limited to engineering matters. He thought deeply on educational, social and metaphysical problems, and devoted much of his time to questions of national defence, both on land and at sea, particularly following his retirement.

In a rambling letter to the 4th Earl of Rosse, dated 17th December 1907, Stoney writes about his ideas for sinking enemy ships by ramming them at high speed with a small fast destroyer loaded with high explosives. He even suggested a small watertight craft so that the two man crew could have some chance of escaping! He had made the suggestion a few years earlier to Charles Parsons, the inventor of the steam turbine and designer of the 'Turbinia'. Stoney concluded his letter by remarking that 'I begin to feel Anno Domini pretty sharply, and have to be very cautious about chills.'

Stoney took a keen interest in both the education and training of professional engineers and was a promoter of the then new concept of extending the benefits of a technical education to the labouring class. In the first part of his Presidential Address to the Institution of Civil Engineers of Ireland, he set forth a number of recommendations for changes in engineering education which were ahead of their time, such as continuous assessment and specialisation. He felt that syllabi were too crammed with peripheral subjects and recommended following the system then in operation in the European Polytechnics of concentrating on gaining competence in a few specific areas of study rather than following a diversified course. However, even today, University courses are largely non-specialist. Stoney also favoured industrial experience between academic years. In the matter of the extension of technical education to the labouring, he felt that the basic theory and use of the lever, pulley, wedge and screw should be taught in all primary schools. Most labourers did not seem to understand the concept of friction, or know how to relieve or mitigate its effects. The Mechanics Institutes in England provided much of the instruction advocated by Stoney, but did not operate in Ireland, with the exception of the industrial area of Belfast.

In addition to being a great engineer, Stoney was a man of wide and varied reading, and was well-known for his sound judgement in letters and in art, possessing a deep theoretical knowledge of music. In social life he was regarded as the most kindly of men, humorous and sociable, and enjoyed a wide circle of friends. As a small example of his humorous trait, his response to a letter to the Board, dated 27th May 1887, from J Wood Aston Co. of Stourbridge is typical. Enclosed with the letter was a drawing of a 'Mooring Swivel', which had been made the wrong size and was surplus to requirements. Stoney's comment written across the bottom of the letter was 'of no use except to hang as (a) pendant from (the) Secretary's watch chain!'

Retirement and closing years

Apart from an attack of lumbago and sciatica during the winter of 1894 'that temporarily floored me', Stoney's very occasional letters to the Board regarding his health indicate a robustness of constitution that complemented his dedication to his work. His ability, coupled with this dedication, enabled him to essentially complete the task of turning the Harbour of Dublin into an efficient deep-water port, thus ensuring its prosperity for many years thereafter.

The following winter saw Stoney, at the age of 67, confined to bed for a few days by his medical adviser, Dr Wallace Beatty, to recover from a bout of influenza and a touch of pleurisy. As Stoney remarked in a letter to the Board: 'I suppose he is right, as so many people get pneumonia after flu and I don't feel quite up to par.'

However, what really affected Bindon's health in a significant way were the events of March 1897. He had been to London on business and, returning from Holyhead to Kingstown on the mail packet steamer Ulster had to wait on Carlisle Pier (Kingstown) for nearly an hour awaiting onward transport. After having spent the night on the boat in a hot place situated over the engines, he caught a chill on the pier, from which he developed a severe bronchial cold. The Ulster was the fastest steamer operating on the crossing and is recorded as having made the crossing between Holyhead and Kingstown on 9th February, 1897 in the record time of 2 hours 26 minutes.

Writing to the Board on St Patrick's Day, 1897, he informed Proud that the doctor had confined him to the house for several days and had 'clapped a fly blister on my left lung and given me a sleeping draught to enable me, if possible, to get a night's rest, a thing I have not had since this day week.' He referred to complications having set in and hoped that remedies will prove effectual.' After the passage of a further week, however, he was advised by a Dr. Walter Smith to go to 'somewhere like Rostrevor for a change in order to get rid of the crackling in his lung.'

Stoney recovered sufficiently to resume his duties in the port, but the following year, after a recurrence of the bronchial condition, took advantage of the terms of the pension provision in the Dublin Port & Docks Act of 1898 (61 & 62 Vic.) and, in a letter to the Board dated 20th December 1898, sought permission to retire.

Section 115 of the 1898 Act provided for superannuation or retirement allowances (pensions) to be granted on the same scale as that to which the retiring employee would have been entitled had they held a similar office for a like period of years in the permanent Civil Service of the State at the same salary and had been retired from such office, i.e. comparability had been established.

The decision to pay Stoney a salary of £2,000 per annum from 1884 until his retirement in 1898 on a pension of £1,333, is a measure of the high value placed on his work by the Board. Early in 1884, he had asked the Board to consider a further increase in his salary and the Board resolved 'that Dr Stoney's salary be increased from £1,500 to £2,000 a year from 1 January, 1884, such £2,000 to be the maximum salary, and to be personal to Dr Stoney, and not to form any precedent for future holders of the office, being given to Dr Stoney in recognition of the great services he has rendered to the Port of Dublin.'

Thus, after forty two and an half years in the service of Dublin Port, Stoney handed over the reins to the engineer who had been his faithful Assistant for 27 years, John Purser Griffith. Although Stoney Road, off East Wall Road near the main railway line to the north, was named in Stoney's honour by a grateful city, it is somewhat surprising to find that he was never offered the Freedom of the City of Dublin, an honour which was to be reserved for Purser Griffith, albeit at the ripe old age of 96.

Stoney lived within the bounds of what is now the Parish of St Bartholemew, but the present church was not completed until 1867. Thus Bindon attended St Mary's Church of Ireland Church in Donnybrook. In his later years, when work at the port had slackened considerably, Bindon found time to become a member of the Select Vestry of the parish. From then on, he served on the vestry every year up until the time of his death in 1909, holding the position of churchwarden in 1887.

On January 23rd, 1909, Bindon learned by cable that his only son, George Bindon, had died the day previous in Australia at his residence at Lindfield in New South Wales. From the Donnybrook Parish Magazine for 1909 we learn that George 'from childhood had been a singularly attractive personality. He was richly endowed with intellectual gifts, which gave promise of a most distinguished career in life, and he was ever good and kind as he was clever.' He was obviously his father's pride and joy and hope for the future. At an early age, George had obtained a high place in the competitive examination for entry to Woolwich College and passed out as an army cadet into the Royal Engineers. After a little while, however, ill-health obliged him to resign his commission. For some years he lived in Australia where the climate in New South Wales seemed to agree with him. I was unable to discover the nature of his illness, but George Bindon's early death at twenty seven years of age affected his father greatly.

So much so that Bindon went into a rapid decline and died at his home at 14 Elgin Road in Dublin on the 5th May, 1909. Bindon Blood Stoney was buried on the 10th May in Mount Jerome Cemetery in Dublin following a funeral service in the Mortuary Chapel, conducted by the Rector of Donnybrook, the Reverend Robert Walsh, D.D., and, a relative, the Reverend Canon Stoney, D.D.

In his address at the conclusion of the service, the Rector summed up Stoney's character in the following manner: 'If rare intellectual attainments, and great worth of character deserve special honour and special notice, the late Dr Stoney is entitled to these, for he held a chief place among those of his contempories (sic) who most deserve honour and respect', and again 'He was not merely a distinguished engineer, one of the chiefs of a great profession, he was a man of wide culture, of varied reading, of remarkable information. He was endowed with intellectual gifts of no common order. These, united to genuine goodness and kindliness of heart, made him a delightful friend and companion.

He had the happy gift of making you feel at your ease with him, when discussing subjects on which he knew more than you. Distinguished by a marked independence of character, possessed of a store of information, his unassuming nature never unduly asserted itself. Any trace of pride of intellect was entirely absent from him; to know him was to love him; to know him well was to love and honour him the more. For deeper in him than his culture was that which gave his friendship its real charm, this was his absolute sincerity and simplicity of character, a more guileless man I never came in contact with. It is too often the inveterate tendency of very clever men to use their great gifts with the object of influencing others for their own purposes. Through the long years I have known our friend, the thing that impressed me as a marked feature of his character was the love of truth, for its own sake, and his ceaseless desire to attain it and promote it because it was the right. He was above all petty aims or devious methods; he was essentially an honest man. In working with him you noticed he always formed an independent judgement on each subject under consideration. If he thought it his duty to take a different view from yours you felt so assured of the sincerity of his motive, that whether with you or against you in counsel, you were glad to have him as a colleague.' Surely a fitting tribute to a great engineer and a great man.

Stoney was regarded as an eminent authority on Port Engineering in the U.K. and was consulted by most of the harbour authorities in Ireland, in spite of the restrictions placed upon him by the Board. His ability as an engineer was universally acknowledged, and his unswerving integrity and love of truth and justice, gained him the esteem of all those who worked under him. As a member of the Board of Dublin Port put it: Stoney was 'most courtly in manner, (and) was one of the old school which was rapidly passing away.' He was a man of high character, upright, and, above all, a good citizen. This ingenious engineer believed passionately in what he was trying to achieve in Dublin Port. Even under trying conditions and with limited funding, he succeeded in completing a series of major construction projects vital to the future development of Dublin.

Right:
St.Mary's Church of Ireland Church, Donnybrook, Dublin 4

Far right:
Grave of B.B.Stoney in Mount Jerome Cemetery, Dublin 6

He was not merely a distinguished engineer, one of the chiefs of a great profession, he was a man of wide culture, of varied reading, of remarkable information. He was endowed with intellectual gifts of no common order. These, united to genuine goodness and kindliness of heart, made him a delightful friend and companion.

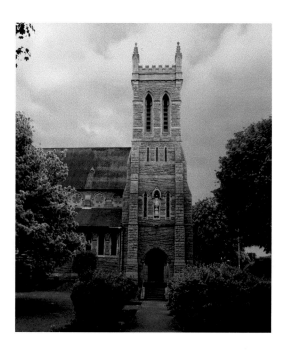

Above:
**Stoney's Diving Bell
as Ireland's smallest
museum, opened 2015**

John Purser Griffith

1848–1938

Purser Griffith's early life and education

Family roots

In 1936, on the occasion of his being made an Honorary Freeman of the City of Dublin, Purser Griffith described himself as being 'a pure Welshman, drawn to Dublin by family ties and friendships. Towards the end of the 18th century several of my relatives left their Welsh homes and came to Ireland to be educated and to earn their bread'. Though thoroughly Welsh on both sides of his family, he spent all his adult life in Dublin and regarded himself as an adopted Irishman. The ties and friendships referred to were those between the Griffith and Purser families.

In 1776, John Purser, who is believed to have been born in Tewkesbury in Gloucestershire, came to Dublin from London to brew porter for James Farrell, who operated a small brewery at Blackpitts in the Liberties. It is said that this John Purser, who died in Cork in 1781, was the first to brew porter in Ireland.

His eldest son, John (1760-1830), who had been born in London, moved to Dublin in 1776 and was trained by his father as a porter brewer. He was appointed Chief Clerk at Guinness's brewery at St James's Gate and later became a partner in the firm. In 1783 he married Dorothea Antisell from Tipperary, by whom he had a son, John, known as John "Secundus" Purser (1783-1858).

John S. Purser succeeded his father at Guinness's and also became a partner and a close and valued friend of the famous brewing family. He had connections in the Welsh border country and was also a frequent visitor to Bristol, where he purchased hops and barley for the brewery in Dublin. In 1808 he married Sarah Smyth (or Smith) of Oswestry, Denbigh in North Wales and had a daughter Sarah, who in 1839 married Richard William Biggs of Devizes in Wiltshire. (Dr Biggs ran a school in the town, which was later to figure prominently in Purser Griffith's early education). They had eight children, the eldest son being known as John "Tertius" Purser (1809-1893).

John T.Purser joined his father in the brewery at St James's Gate in 1824 and was made head brewer on the death of his father in 1858. He also became a partner in the firm. As a child he had been tutored with the Guinness boys in the same classroom. Much to the annoyance of his father, who was a convinced Baptist, he embraced the Moravian faith in 1831, when he was welcomed into the congregation of the Moravian Church in Bishop Street in Dublin, subsequently becoming a prominent member and generous benefactor of that church. The Moravians are a Protestant sect, founded in Saxony by emigrants from Moravia (now part of the Czech Republic), holding views derived from the Hussites and accepting the Bible as the only source of faith. The Hussites were members or followers of the movement begun by John Huss, a Bohemian religious and nationalist reformer who died in 1415.

Three years later, in 1834, John T.Purser married Anna Benigna Fridlezius, daughter of Rev. Jens Fridlezius, and went to live for a time at his father's new residence, Rathmines Castle before moving to a house of his own at Cross Avenue in Blackrock. Fridlezius, born in Sweden in 1750, was Warden of the Gracehill Moravian community near Ballymena in county Antrim, where he died in 1816. He led Robert Mallet (1810-1881) and John Tertius Purser on a European Grand Tour. Anna's mother, Anna Benigna Craven, was also a Moravian, born at Fulneck in Yorkshire in 1759. Their daughter took her mother's names and in 1871 married John (later Sir John) Purser Griffith.

Purser Griffith inherited Rathmines Castle from his father, but the property was let for some years to a Col.Radcliffe, and Purser did not move in until around 1875. The castle, built about 1820 by a Col.Wynne, was to remain in the family until about 1965, when it was sold to the Representative Body of the Church of Ireland to serve as accommodation for a college of education. The castle was subsequently demolished to make way for the present complex of buildings.

Right:
John Tertius Purser

Far right:
Rev. William Griffith

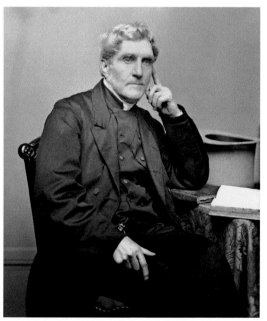

In 1776, John Purser, who is believed to have been born in Tewkesbury in Gloucestershire, came to Dublin from London to brew porter for James Farrell, who operated a small brewery at Blackpitts in the Liberties. It is said that this John Purser, who died in Cork in 1781, was the first to brew porter in Ireland.

Dublin Port Chief Engineers
John Purser Griffith (1848-1938)

Both John T. Purser and his father were close friends of the Rev. William Griffith, the Congregational Minister at Holyhead. Through the Moravian church, John T. would have met William's future wife, Alicia Evans, and her Moravian aunts. Indeed, he may well have been instrumental in arranging a meeting of the young couple who were later to marry and have a son, John Purser Griffith.

Purser Griffith, in turn, also became an influential member of the Moravian Church, and took much pride in his Welsh-Moravian forbears. His great-great grandfather, William Griffith (1719-82), was a well-read farmer from Drys-y- Coed in the Beddgelert district of Caernarvonshire. William was born in 1719, and married in 1753 Alice Ellis. Their home was the centre for the Moravian Mission in North Wales, five of his daughters becoming Moravian workers in Dublin. One of his daughters married a Mr Evans and had a daughter Alicia. Alicia came to Dublin as a child and was educated by an aunt. She joined the Moravian church in Dublin, assisted in the school, and became a governess in Lord Somerville's family. She later spent some time with her Moravian aunts in Bristol where, in 1843, she married the Rev. William Griffith (1801-1881).

William Griffith was by then the minister in charge of the Welsh Calvinist Church at Holyhead and a renowned preacher and hymn-writer. The younger son of John Griffith (1752-1818), he was born at Glan-yr-afon, Llanfaglen, Caernarvonshire in 1801 and lived in that district before pursuing theological studies at a college in Carmarthen. Leaving college in 1822, he boarded ship at Tenby for Dublin (a steamship service from Bristol to Dublin had commenced service in May of that year, for the summer season only, calls being made at Tenby and Wexford on the outward and at Liverpool on the return voyage).

Following a short visit to Dublin, William travelled in the Royal Sovereign to Holyhead to be ordained a minister in the Congregational Church. At the time, land travel between southern and northern parts Wales was difficult owing to the intervening mountains and it was quite common to make such journeys by sea via Dublin.

When William answered the call to Holyhead, the congregation numbered only thirteen souls, and there was no church building. He raised the money to build the present Tabernacle (completed in 1824 and extended in 1884 in his memory) and was the pastor there for nearly sixty years, during which time the congregation rose to around 500. He is buried, alongside his wife and young daughter, at the entrance to the Tabernacle. William Griffith remained at Holyhead for the rest of his life, refusing ministries in other parts of England and Wales. His long ministry was of great importance in the history of Independency in Anglesey, he himself becoming one of the leaders of the denomination in North Wales. His own connections with Moravianism are of interest.

His mother was a niece of the aforementioned William Griffith (1719-82), and his association with that family was further strengthened by his marriage to Alicia. The marriage was solemnised at Bristol Moravian Chapel, and the bride's aunt, Mary Griffith, a Moravian "labouress", came to live for a while with the newly married couple at Holyhead, where she died in 1847. On 5th October 1848 Alicia gave birth to their only son John. When John was six years of age, he and his elder sister Mary Dorothy both contracted virulent 'scarletina'. Sadly his sister died from the disease, but the young John survived. As a result of their close ties with the Purser family in Dublin, the young Griffith was given the second name "Purser". His mother Alicia died on 21st March, 1865, a few months before Purser Griffith entered Trinity College in Dublin to study civil engineering.

Purser Griffith's father was a renowned evangelistic preacher and regarded by his contemporaries as a very holy man. He was a good mathematician, a fine linguist, and had a good taste for music and the arts. These traits were passed on in varying measure to his son, who was also proficient at mathematics and had an excellent command of language. Purser Griffith's interest in music led him to become organist at the Moravian Church in Dublin and a leading figure in the organisation of the Feis Ceol.

Purser Griffith's father was a renowned evangelistic preacher and regarded by his contemporaries as a very holy man. He was a good mathematician, a fine linguist, and had a good taste for music and the arts. These traits were passed on in varying measure to his son, who was also proficient at mathematics and had an excellent command of language.

Congregational Church at Holyhead, completed in 1884

Education

In 1861, at the age of thirteen, Purser Griffith was sent by his parents to a boys' preparatory school in Devizes in Wiltshire. The town had, from the late eighteenth century, quite a reputation as an educational centre. No fewer than sixteen different houses in Long Street were at one time or another used to house centres of tuition and there were many others in the town. One of the best known establishments was that run by Dr Richard William Biggs (1816-83). The school was located originally in High Street, Devizes, but by 1830 had moved to Lansdowne House in Long Street and later moved to Wilsford House, also in Long Street. The school aimed to prepare boys for university and offered a wide curriculum, including Geometry, Algebra, Latin and German.

Richard William Biggs was born in Dublin in 1816 and attended Trinity College Dublin, from where he graduated in 1839 with an MA degree. He was awarded a BA degree from the University of London and later received an LL.D from the University of Dublin. On the 17th July 1839, he married Sarah Purser (not the artist), the eldest daughter of John "Secundus" Purser, whom he had met in his college days in Dublin, and moved to Devizes to assist his father in the running of the school and to take over much of the teaching. Many of the boarders who came to Dr Bigg's school were from Ireland, including, as we have noted, John Purser Griffith. Purser Griffith's father may have been influenced in his decision to send his son to Devizes by his friendship with Sarah Bigg's brother, John Tertius Purser. In a letter to Purser Griffith dated 17th September, 1863, his mother referred to "young John Purser" and urged her son to emulate the Pursers who "have been hard-working men."

Following his two years at school in Devizes, his parents arranged for Purser Griffith to attend the famous Moravian school at Fulneck in Yorkshire, where his headmaster was Joseph Willey. In 1750, the Moravians began building a settlement on a steep hillside near the village of Pudsey near Leeds. The school, named after an earlier school at Fulneck in Moravia (now part of the Czech Republic), was opened in 1753 and is still flourishing. In 1865 Purser Griffith left Fulneck to enter Trinity College in Dublin. His later distinctions in professional and public life made him one of the best-known Old Boys of the school, and he was the principal founder of the Fulneck School War Memorial Fund, and in other ways gave his continued support to his old school.

Fulneck School, Leeds

Holyhead harbour

When not at school, Purser Griffith spent much of his time in the company of his parents at home in Holyhead. This was during the time of the building of the great harbour of refuge and the young Purser Griffith would have looked on in wonderment as the engineers and workmen battled with the forces of nature to painstakingly extend the great breakwaters into the sea.

When the bridging of the Menai Straits by the Chester & Holyhead Railway became no longer a matter of doubt, it was decided by the government that Holyhead was the most suitable location for a harbour of refuge to accommodate the ships providing a packet or mail service to Ireland. Of several schemes that had been proposed up to that time, that suggested by James Meadows Rendel (1799-1856) was accepted and, in August 1845, he was requested by the Lords of the Treasury to provide detailed plans and estimates for a new harbour. His report was received in December of that year and an Act to enable the necessary land to be purchased received royal assent on 22nd July, 1847.

Rendel's plan consisted of northern and eastern breakwaters, together creating a sheltered roadstead of around 400 acres in addition to the 276 acres of inner harbour, and a packet pier within the enclosed area. Work commenced on the northern breakwater in 1847, the year before Purser Griffith was born at nearby Holyhead. Rendel died in 1856 and the work was completed under Sir John Hawkshaw (1811-91), assisted by Harrison Hayter (1825-98). The northern breakwater eventually reached a length of 7,860 feet. It was built with stone brought down by a railway from quarries on Holyhead Mountain and was under continuous construction until 1873, although most of the stone had been deposited prior to 1863. The superstructure and head of the breakwater with its lighthouse was constructed between 1860 and 1873. The new breakwater was officially opened by the Prince of Wales in August 1873.

The young Purser Griffith would have become increasingly conscious of the significant feat of marine engineering being undertaken on his parent's doorstep. He would have heard many of the explosions as over one thousand mines were fired to extract some of the seven million tons of stone required to complete this monumental task. The importance of the harbour may be judged from reports that, in 1863 alone, more than 3,500 vessels entered the harbour for shelter or for unloading. In his paper 'Engineering Reminiscences', published by the Institution of Civil Engineers of Ireland (ICEI) in 1936, Purser Griffith stated that he was 'a great believer in the influence of environment in determining the course of a man's life, and the choice of his employment or profession.'

One of his earliest memories was of William Provis (1792-1870), Telford's chief assistant and resident engineer on the Conway and Menai suspension bridges, and the road from Holyhead to Chester. Provis lived in Holyhead near to the Griffith's home and was, as Purser Griffith said, 'an ideal gentleman of my childhood.' Purser Griffith was also acquainted with the engineers, contractors and workmen carrying out construction work down the road at the harbour. He considered that they had greatly influenced his decision to enter the civil engineering profession. The strong family connections with Dublin, where a School of Civil Engineering had been established at Trinity College in 1841, led Purser Griffith to decide to enrol at the college in the autumn of 1865. Following the death of his mother in March of that year, his father William seems to have become even more absorbed in following his evangelistic mission in North Wales. However, in June 1866, he suffered sunstroke whilst preaching in the open-air at Pwllheli and was incapacitated and unable to carry on his ministry for almost four years.

Published by Brook & Roberts, London, Nov. 1874.

HOLYHEAD BREAKWATER & HARBOUR OF REFUGE.

**Holyhead Breakwater
& Harbour of Refuge.
Published by Brook
& Roberts, 1874**

The young Purser Griffith
would have become
increasingly conscious
of the significant feat of
marine engineering being
undertaken on his parent's
doorstep. He would have
heard many of the explosions
as over one thousand mines
were fired to extract some
of the seven million tons of
stone required to complete
this monumental task.

Engineering studies

During this time, Purser Griffith was pursuing his engineering course at Trinity College Dublin, which at that time was under the direction of Professor Samuel Downing. The course was of three years duration, at the end of which successful candidates were awarded a Licence in Civil Engineering (the Bachelor's degree was not instituted until 1870). During his first year, Purser Griffith studied Mathematics, Theoretical Mechanics and Chemistry, passing the year with an overall average mark of 46%. His second year, in which he studied Physics, Practical Mechanics and Drawing, resulted in an improved mark of 54%, a possible indication of his later aptitude for the mechanical and electrical aspects of engineering. The final year was occupied with lectures and practical work in Practical Engineering, Geology and Drawing. Purser Griffith achieved third place in his final examination in a class of 29 and received a Special Certificate (Honours) for his answering in Practical Mechanics and Physics.

Marriage

In November 1871, Purser Griffith, then only 23 years of age, married Anna Benigna Fridlezius, nine years his senior and the only daughter of his father's life-long friend, John "Tertius" Purser. The marriage took place at the Moravian Church in Bishop Street in Dublin, the reception being held at Rathmines Castle. The couple moved into "Greenane", a substantial house in Temple Road in Rathmines. The house was probably part of Anna's dowry as her husband's commencing salary was only £150 per annum at the time as an assistant engineer at Dublin Port. It is located in the grounds of Trinity Hall, part of the original Rathmines Castle estate.

On the death of Anna's father in 1893, Rathmines Castle passed to her brother John (1835-1903), who continued to reside there until his death in 1903. In that same year, Purser Griffith moved into the "Castle" with his wife and daughter Alice (1876-1965). Their elder son, John William (1875-1936), was married and continued to live at "Greenane" until his death in 1936. Purser Griffith's other son, Frederick (1878-1939), resided nearby at "Gwynant" in Temple Gardens until his death in 1939.

Far left:
Greenane, Temple Road, Rathmines, Dublin, the first home of the Purser-Griffiths

Left:
Anna Benigna Purser (Lady Griffith), painted by Sarah Purser, c1889

Assistant to Bindon Blood Stoney

Appointment as assistant to Stoney

On leaving college in 1868, Purser Griffith became a pupil of Bindon Blood Stoney at Dublin Port. In a letter to Proud, the Secretary to the Dublin Port & Docks Board, in 1899, Purser Griffith noted that it was an almost universal custom to take pupils in the leading engineering offices, and considered it the best method for a young engineer to acquire knowledge in any special branch of his profession. As a boy in Holyhead, Purser Griffith became friends with Anthony George Lyster, whose father George Fosberry Lyster was one of the assistant engineers working on the Holyhead harbour project. In due course Anthony succeeded his father as Chief Engineer of the Mersey Docks & Harbour Board at Liverpool. Purser Griffith later sent his eldest son, John William, who had graduated from the engineering school in Trinity College in 1898, to Lyster's office and paid him a fee of 500 guineas for the privilege. His son later became assistant to his father at Dublin Port, taking over as Engineer-in-Chief in 1913. Two signed drawings by Purser Griffith in the Irish Architectural Archives are from this period. (IAA Drawings Nos. 85/166.1,2,3) They are dated September and October 1868 respectively, one being of a three-span masonry arch bridge over the river Liffey, the other of a single masonry arch bridge over Conyngham Road in Dublin. These may well have been test pieces completed when Purser Griffith was commencing his time as a pupil with Stoney. A further undated drawing shows the proposed alterations to the profile of Essex (later Grattan) Bridge, the reconstruction of which Stoney had designed in 1865.

Early in 1870, Purser Griffith secured a position at £50 per annum as one of a number of assistant county surveyors with Antrim County Council working on road projects. The county surveyor, Alexander Tate (1823-1887), had taken over in 1861 from Charles Lanyon (1813-1889). Tate had previously held the post of county surveyor in Dublin between 1855 and 1861 with responsibility for the Northern Division, during which time he acted as Hon. Secretary of the ICEI, a task which he handed over to Stoney on transferring to Antrim. No doubt encouraged by Tate and by Stoney, Purser Griffith was soon elected to membership of the ICEI and was, in due course, to play an important part in its activities, becoming President in 1887. Purser Griffith remained in Antrim until April 1871.

Shortly after the re-organisation of the port administration in 1867, when the Dublin Port & Docks Board replaced the Ballast Board, the Board appointed a Harbour Improvement Committee 'to enquire into and report on the means to be adopted to meet the requirements for the better accommodation of the trade of the Port.' Proposed works included rebuilding much of the north and south quays, the extension of the North Wall, the construction of a second graving dock and the rebuilding of Carlisle (O'Connell) Bridge.

The scale of the projects envisaged called for extra staff, in particular, the appointment of young engineers to assist Stoney. Purser Griffith clearly came to be regarded as Stoney's right-hand man and, by the time of Mann's retirement in 1881, Purser Griffith's duties were 'to assist in making surveys, plans, specifications and estimates; to set out, measure and inspect works; assist in office correspondence, preparation of reports and management of the Department, and to represent the Engineer in his absence.' Between 1871 and 1898, Purser Griffith and Stoney shared the responsibility for all the engineering work in the port and were assisted at times by a number of young engineers taken on for short periods as pupils.

Stoney was already acquainted with the young Purser Griffith and had obviously been impressed enough with his potential to offer him a permanent position. This he gladly accepted, it being an ambition, which he had nurtured from his childhood days in Holyhead, to work on the building of a great harbour or port. And so began a long and fruitful period of professional co-operation and close friendship between these two adopted Dubliners.

When Purser Griffith entered the service of the port authorities on 4th April 1871, there were only two shipping berths outside of the Custom House (Docks) where a vessel drawing 12 feet of water could lie afloat at all states of

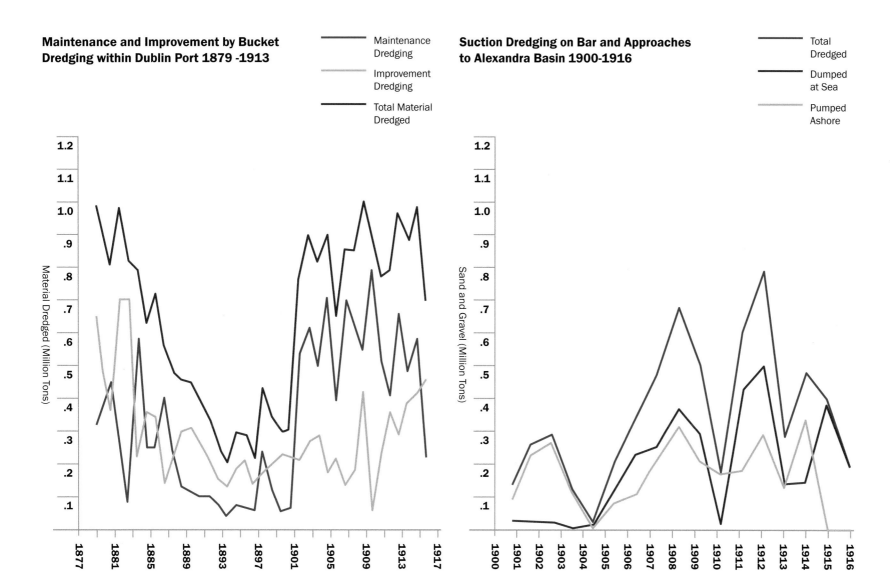

Maintenance and Improvement by Bucket Dredging within Dublin Port 1879 -1913

— Maintenance Dredging
— Improvement Dredging
— Total Material Dredged

Suction Dredging on Bar and Approaches to Alexandra Basin 1900-1916

— Total Dredged
— Dumped at Sea
— Pumped Ashore

the tide. In 1869 the contractor William Doherty had commenced the task of rebuilding the eastern section of Sir John Rogerson's Quay and, by November 1871, some 850 feet of quay wall had been rebuilt. Meanwhile, on the north side of the river, in May of that year, Stoney was supervising the laying of the first of his large monolithic concrete blocks to form the North Wall Extension as part of the creation of Alexandra Basin. The painstaking rebuilding of the North Quays had begun as early as 1864, but would not be completed under Purser Griffith's direction until 1907.

Purser Griffith would have been well aware of Stoney's great project and was obviously excited at the possibility of becoming involved. Thus, when the call came, Purser Griffith jumped at the chance. It turned out to be one of the most important decisions of his life and Stoney was also equally fortunate in being able to recruit someone with such potential. The partnership was to last for 27 years, both men dedicating themselves to the formidable task of creating and maintaining, with limited financial resources, a deep-water port for the city of Dublin.

Shortly following his appointment, Purser Griffith was admitted to membership of the ICEI on the 23rd November 1871. His sponsors were Samuel Downing, the then Professor of Civil Engineering at Trinity College, and W.G.Strype, the chief mechanical engineer at Grendon's works in Dundalk. The Chairman of the interviewing committee was his boss, Bindon

Stoney, who was President of the ICEI at the time. Purser Griffith, like Stoney, was a great supporter of engineering professional bodies and served for many years on the Council of both the Dublin and London civil engineering institutions. He became President of the ICEI during the session 1887-88 at the age of 39.

Not long after joining Stoney at Dublin Port, Purser Griffith visited the Port of Hamburg on the invitation of the Chief Engineer, Dalmann. He was impressed by the rapid turnaround of shipping at the port, which was well equipped with steam cranes, railways, sheds, etc. On later visits, he found that the steam cranes had been replaced by hydraulic and, later still, electric cranes. Dalmann claimed to be able to accommodate more shipping per lineal foot of quay than any British port. Purser Griffith examined the position in Dublin and realised that, although coastal shipping spent few days in port, ocean-going vessels often spent four to six weeks tied up in port alongside expensive quaysides. He realised that quick turnaround of ships was essential, but that this could not be achieved without mechanical handling equipment, such as cranes, to a large extent replacing manual dock labour. However, the first priority was to provide deep-water access to the port for larger vessels, and it was not until the early 1900s that moves were made to provide a range of mechanised facilities to speed up the handling of cargoes.

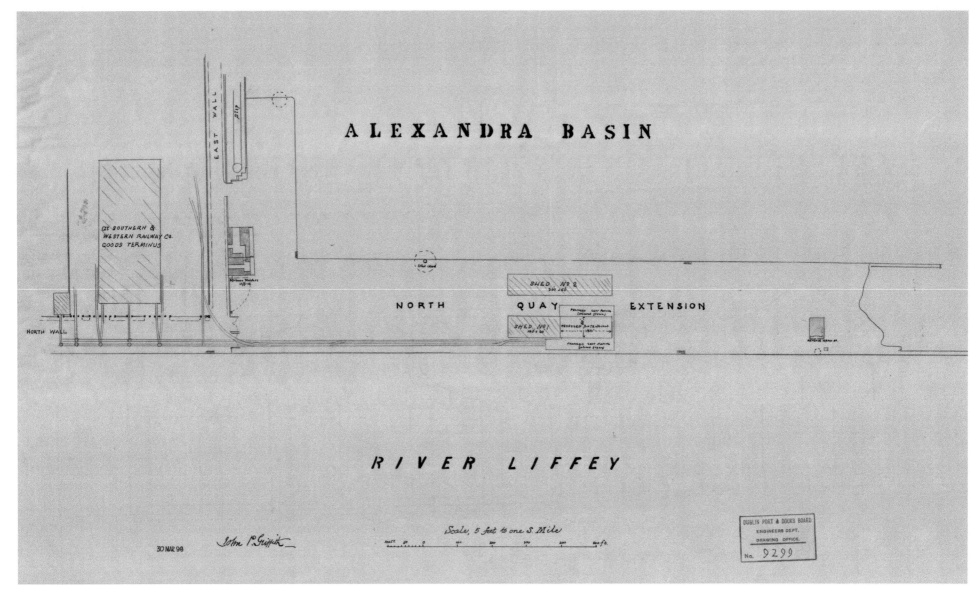

ALEXANDRA BASIN

NORTH QUAY EXTENSION

RIVER LIFFEY

Above:
**Alexandra Basin, North
Quay Extension, 1898**

Opposite page:
**Shipping at North Quay
Extension with 100 ton
crane in distance**

Developments at Dublin Port

Addressing the opening meeting of the 1914-15 session of the Dublin
University Engineering Society in Trinity College, Purser Griffith took
the opportunity to record the development of the Port of Dublin in the years
since the Act of 1707, which set up the Ballast Office to levy tonnage dues
and use these to improve the approach channel in the river to the quays. The
development of the Port of Dublin has been ably recounted by Gilligan in
his history of Dublin Port published in 1988. Purser Griffith quite naturally
concentrated on the period during which he was employed by the Board,
namely 1871 to 1913. During this time many important improvements were
made to the port, including the provision of deep-water quays along the
north and south banks of the river, the extension of the North Wall to form
Alexandra Basin, additional lighthouses, a major dredging programme, the
electrification of the port, and the provision of facilities for the handling and
storage of oil products. Purser Griffith formed many personal friendships
with distinguished engineers who visited the Port to view the work on the
North Wall Extension and these contacts were to prove useful in his later
consulting work for a number of port authorities, including Liverpool and
Hull.

An account of the major achievement of Bindon Stoney in creating the
deep-water Alexandra Basin has already been described in Chapter Four. It is
clear that Purser Griffith contributed significantly to the successful outcome
of this project and other port developments, such as the reconstruction of the
river-side berths and a number of bridges. Reporting in 1912, on the occasion
of Purser Griffith's proposed retirement from Dublin Port, the Irish Builder
& Engineer remarked 'During the actual administration of Sir John Griffith
himself as Chief Engineer, no works of great public fame have been done,
but this may be said to be due solely to the fact that as the right hand of so
eminent a man as Dr Stoney, he had the largest share in the carrying out of
the great works, and if his works since have been less known to public fame,
they have not been the less important.' However, Purser Griffith was allowed
in due course to develop a wider role as a consultant outside of his port
duties, whereas Stoney was expressly prevented from so doing by the terms
of his agreement with the board. When his salary was increased to £1,500
per annum in September 1872, Stoney undertook in return 'to continue to
give his professional services exclusively to the port.' This resulted in Purser
Griffith becoming more widely recognised in the profession.

Evidence of Purser Griffith's intimate involvement with a wide range of engineering works at the port during Stoney's period as Engineer-in-Chief is to be found in his many papers published in the Transactions of the ICEI Between 1877 and 1895, he wrote no fewer than twelve papers, in addition to his Presidential Address, on such diverse subjects as the rebuilding of Essex (Grattan) Bridge and Standard Tests for Portland Cement. Of particular importance was his 1889 paper on Standard Specifications in which he stressed the need for uniform standards for all engineering materials. The general practice at the time was for each engineer to specify their own standards and there was a bewildering variation. He felt that one of the functions of the ICEI should be to promote the adoption of standard tests for various construction materials and proof tests for completed structures. He had been impressed by what he had seen in Germany and had translated the German standards for ironwork and cement into English, these forming a valuable appendix to his paper. The setting up of standard specifications for engineering materials was a great advance, both for manufacturers and users, and did much to eliminate the bewildering variations in specifications. His two papers on Portland Cement were, in the opinion of Pierce Purcell, 'so ably written, and deal in such an exact manner with the properties and testing of cement, that they were far in advance of the ideas then held in Great Britain.' Purser Griffith's papers exhibit, not only a deep knowledge of engineering principles and practice, but a considerable flair for stimulating debate on the important issues of the day. He had a strong command of language, although his papers were written in the somewhat verbose style of earlier generations.

Purser Griffith's presidential address to the ICEI, delivered in the Museum Building in Trinity College in 1887, was wide-ranging in its review of the state of the profession and engineering works. He regretted that the architects had found it necessary to go their own way (in 1844) as he considered architecture to be 'but a branch of civil engineering'. When speaking about education and training, he identified the most essential attributes of an engineer as 'common sense, power of observation, and tact in the management of men.'

Nearly 50 years later, Professor Rishworth, who had been Chief Engineer on the Shannon Scheme, in a warning to parents, stated 'that unless (your) son has a creative imagination, a distinct mathematical bias, capacity for work, a good physique, and a personality that would get on with and control men, he should seek some other calling.' Rishworth considered that 'success in the profession does not depend upon one's knowledge of engineering alone, a capacity for getting on with people, otherwise tact, a faculty for organisation and hard work are attributes which lead to its attainment.'

Purser Griffith believed that it was 'an important duty of engineers to unite efficiency and economy in all their designs. Failure of works on economic grounds brings discredit on our profession, second only to failures from structural defects.' Referring to recent progress in engineering, he mentioned the telephone as 'a time-saving instrument that, but for the convenience of rapid communication, would be expelled from many an office as an unqualified nuisance and rude companion.' He did, however, acknowledge that telephonic communication had greatly increased the safety of diving operations in the port.

Purser Griffith concluded his address with a message for young men entering the engineering profession, which I think is worth quoting in full as it is an indication of Purser Griffith's considerable commitment to furthering the future status of the profession. 'My object in dwelling so much upon the history of our profession has been to stimulate you to assist in making its future worthy of its past. I also wish to encourage young men entering upon their work, and to awaken their enthusiasm. With none have I more sympathy, and I would say to them – Do not be discouraged by anything you have heard this evening, but if your heart is in your work go on fearlessly. To ensure success you must, however, be enthusiasts. It will not do to enter the profession merely because it appears a gentlemanly occupation. If you join it from such motives you may expect failure. Remember you are taking your commission in the constructive army of the world, and, as in the military service, much of your success will turn on your becoming distinguished as leaders of men. Study engineering biography, and you will find that the most eminent engineers have been those who possessed the power of gathering around them men thoroughly devoted and loyal to their interests. Let it be your endeavour, in whatever position you are placed, to surround yourselves with such a body-guard. Whether as assistant or executive engineers strive to make yourselves respected by those under you for your personal as well as your professional worth. Let them learn to look up to you as their counsellor and leader in all cases of difficulty. The progress of engineering science is now so rapid that it is no easy matter for men whose days are fully occupied with professional engagements, to keep themselves informed of the advances which are being made. Yet this is necessary, and you must not shrink from the labour it entails. To ensure a successful career you must keep in touch with the most recent discoveries and improvements in the art of construction, so as to be able to utilise them as occasion may require. If possible, travel, and visit engineering works of importance; by doing so your views will be enlarged and local prejudices corrected, while a wider personal acquaintance with engineers will increase your interest in, and attachment to, the honourable profession which you have joined.'

Dublin Port Chief Engineers
John Purser Griffith (1848-1938)

Griffith becomes Engineer-in-Chief

Engineer-in-Chief

Purser Griffith, referring to the work at Dublin Port, drew attention to the injurious effect on the port finances of the construction placed on the law of measurement of shipping tonnage in 1879 by the High Court and the later interpretation by the Royal Commission on Tonnage in 1881. As a result, revenue had fallen sharply and led to cut backs in port maintenance and a slowing of developmental work.

Stoney's last report to the Dublin Port & Docks Board makes it quite clear that by 1897, as a result of the lack of resources, very little was happening on the engineering front. Even maintenance dredging had been reduced to around one third of what it had been in the 1870s, but suction dredging had been introduced by Purser Griffith in 1895 and was set to expand significantly under his direction. Earlier, in 1892, Purser Griffith had applied for the position of harbour engineer at Belfast and Stoney had provided him with a very flattering testimonial. However, the job went to George Giles and Purser Griffith continued instead to bide his time until Stoney's retirement in 1898.

Some months before Purser Griffith took over at Dublin Port, an agreement was entered into between the Board and the Anglo-American Oil Company for a lease of 8½ acres of land to the east of the graving dock for an oil storage depot, consisting of storage tanks and ancillary buildings. In addition a barrel factory was erected to supply barrels for the company's British and Irish trade. A temporary deep-water timber jetty (Alexandra Wharf) was constructed at the company's expense and the berth and approaches dredged. Alexandra Road was also extended eastwards. The first large tank steamer discharged its cargo of oil in February 1899.

In 1898 the Dublin Port & Docks Board was reconstituted and took office in January 1899, the same month that Purser Griffith formally took over from Stoney, who had retired on health grounds. The board now consisted of the Lord Mayor, six members appointed by the Corporation, and twenty-one elective members, twelve of whom represented the traders and nine the shipping interests. In compliance with the Board's instructions, Purser Griffith reported on what engineering works he considered were likely to be required within the following three to five years. He felt that the most pressing need was the completion of a channel with a depth of 20 feet at standard low water (LWOST) from the North Wall out to sea across the Bar. This was to make Dublin Port more suitable for the overseas trade. Purser Griffith recommended the acquisition of a new suction hopper-dredger and a tug, both of which were provided in due course by the Board. Reclamation and quay reconstruction were amongst other projects listed. The most noticeable defect was the lack of public cargo handling equipment. He felt that Dublin Port possessed exceptional advantages as a distribution centre, but could not compete for trade with other ports without being adequately equipped.

In the Port Bill of 1902, immediately following the revival of shipbuilding in Dublin, powers were obtained to expend £209,000 on the construction of a second graving dock. The Board's failure to increase their revenue, however, prevented any progress being made in that direction and it was not until 1957 that No.2 graving dock was completed. Following an adverse report by an investigating sub-committee, Purser Griffith pointed out to the Board that 'nothing could be worse or more wasteful than stopping works in progress.' In particular, he was concerned about the fate of the North Wall improvement works and the maintenance of the navigation channel across the Bar. However, he did agree that no further works of extension or improvement should be undertaken until the Board had taken steps to generate adequate revenue.

Right and far right:
Construction of Alexandra Quay West employing the 1,500 ton dredger, the Sandpiper.

Opposite page:
The Sandpiper, c1930

Harbour dredging

On taking over from Stoney, Purser Griffith had reorganised the dredging operations and employed the Board's first suction dredger (introduced 1895) to straighten and widen the channel on the south side of the port to the east of Pigeon House Fort. Over half a million tons of fine sand were dredged and conveyed to sea. However, maintenance dredging in other parts of the port suffered from the constant interruptions from shipping and proved to be a heavy drain on the financial resources of the Board. Following complaints about the condition of the navigable channel in the river and across the bar, a hydrographic survey was carried out by Capt. George Pirie, R.N., an experienced naval survey officer. The results of the survey were subsequently published by the Admiralty as the official chart of the harbour. The survey showed that the warnings given to the Board by Purser Griffith and his fellow officers as to the need for a more vigorous dredging policy were warranted and that the additions to dredging plant had been fully justified. It was found that the North Bull had encroached across the approach channel through the Bar since the previous survey in 1889.

Plans to contract for the building of a new suction hopper dredger fell through due to high steel prices. Instead, a dredging contract was placed with the Dutch firm of Kalis & Co. of Sliedrecht to remove some 750,000 tons of sand from the Bar and for pumping a portion of this ashore at the discretion of the engineer. In the event, around 90% of the total was pumped ashore to the north of Alexandra Basin, the remainder being dumped at sea. Purser Griffith was generally against any excessive reclamation within the port area as he felt that such reclamation reduced the tidal capacity on which scour across the Bar depended. He did, however, admit that the channel across the Bar could be maintained by regular suction dredging.

Kalis were invited to extend their contract, but declined, and the Board decided to acquire their own dredger. They placed a contract with the Dutch firm of Smit & Zoon of Kinderdijk for a new suction dredger (for delivery in July, 1904) and an additional tug (the Anna Liffey) from the Dublin Dockyard Co. The 1,500 ton dredger, named the Sandpiper, was specially designed and built for dredging on the Bar and worked in that capacity until 1909, when a channel depth of 20 feet was achieved. Purser Griffith recommended that maintenance of this channel would continue to require considerable dredging in consequence of the washing in of sand from the North Bull, but his opinion fell on deaf ears.

Left:
A construction gang with their foreman

Right:
Workers on the crane barge

Below:
Dublin Port Board members on a tour of inspection of the works c.1900

Dublin Port Chief Engineers
John Purser Griffith (1848-1938)

Left:
Rebuilding of North Quays c.1900

Below:
Construction workers with their tools

By 1907, all the South and North Quays had been substantially replaced with deep-water masonry walls, a total length of 8,326 feet of shipping berths. In the case of the South Quays between Butt Bridge and the Grand Canal Dock at Ringsend, in 1870 the foreshore of the river was dry at low water for the entire length of these quays.

As there were no further borrowing powers to continue the work, dredging over the Bar was discontinued and the Sandpiper was used instead to dredge the approach channel to Alexandra Basin, and in 1916 was laid up until after WW1 by order of the Board. Smit & Zoon also constructed a model of the Sandpiper, which is on permanent display in the Port Centre.

In the Spring of 1900, it was decided to commence the reconstruction of the North Wall Quays in order to provide deep-water berths for the cross-channel steamers to enable them to operate timetables free of tidal restrictions. Despite delays due to slow delivery of plant, by August the first length of coffer dam had been closed and dewatered. The Engineer's Notebooks kept by Purser Griffith chronicle in detail the painstaking work of rebuilding and include meticulous coloured plans indicating the progress of the works with the completion dates for each section between 1900 and 1907. This work, carried out behind coffer dams, entailed the removal of the timber wharves in front of the original quay walls, and the provision of mass concrete foundations to support new masonry quay walls. Purser Griffith built a small electrical plant to provide power for the cranes, pumps, concrete mixers and lighting associated with the reconstruction work at the North Wall berths. Also by 1907, all the South and North Quays had been substantially replaced with deep-water masonry walls, a total length of 8,326 feet of shipping berths. In the case of the South Quays between Butt Bridge and the Grand Canal Dock at Ringsend, in 1870 the foreshore of the river was dry at low water for the entire length of these quays. Following their reconstruction, vessels could sail from them at all states of the tide. Thus, the Port of Dublin could, by 1912, be described no longer as a tidal port.

Dredging Hopper Barge No.8 at work in Dublin Bay.

Electrification of the port

At the beginning of the twentieth century, Belfast was more popular with ship-owners, because of the excessive time taken to discharge cargoes at Dublin, where there was an almost total lack of mechanical cargo handling equipment provided by the port authority. Purser Griffith had already witnessed what could be done at Hamburg and other major ports and set about providing several portal cranes of 10 ton capacity along the quaysides. In 1903, tenders were invited for a much heavier lifting crane of 100 ton capacity, the tender of Vereinigte Maschinenfabrik Augsburg und Maschinenbaugesellschaft Nurnberg A.G. being accepted. Electrical equipment was to be supplied by Siemens.

The foundations for the crane were prepared by port engineering staff at the end of the North Wall Extension and were impressive, consisting of 3,500 tons of concrete supported on 110 piles driven to a depth of 40 feet. The crane, which became a noted Dublin landmark, rose some 80 feet above the quayside, and was erected under Purser Griffith's supervision. Installation and testing were completed in July 1905 and electricity was eventually supplied from the Board's new power station, but temporarily from a small steam turbine plant.

As provided for in the 1902 Port Act, Purser Griffith proceeded to adopt electrical equipment throughout the port area. As a reliable supply of electricity could not be obtained from Dublin Corporation, the Board decided to proceed with the construction of their own power station. This was located at the cross berth near to the present port offices. In October 1905, a contract was placed with C.A. Parsons of Newcastle-upon-Tyne. The plant consisted of three steam turbines coupled directly to continuous current dynamos, each dynamo giving a normal output of 200KW at 500V. The plant was commissioned in 1907 and the electrification of the port area was thus made possible. Apart from the conversion to electrical power of many of the cargo handling devices (e.g. the ten portal cranes), there was a marked improvement in the operation of the port as electric lighting allowed for the continuous working of ships resulting in reduced turnaround times.

At the point where the Royal Canal enters the river Liffey at the North Wall to the west of the East Link Bridge, Purser Griffith designed and supervised the erection in 1912 of twin lifting bridges to replace a rolling drawbridge. He based his design on that previously patented in 1893 by William Scherzer of Chicago. It is possible that Purser Griffith became acquainted with Scherzer's patent when visiting the Exposition in Chicago the same year. The advantage of the twin bridges, which were operated electrically, was that the stoppage of quay traffic when vessels needed to enter or leave the canal system was reduced to a few minutes by alternately raising and lowering each bridge during the locking procedure.

As Purser Griffith remarked in 1908, 'there is little doubt that, as the value of electric appliances becomes understood and appreciated, additional demands will be made on the Board for an extension of their electrical system throughout the Port.' In Syren and Shipping Illustrated, published 12 July 1911, Purser Griffith was described as having '......effected something like a revolution in the accommodation and facilities of the port...during the time that (he) has been chief engineer of the port, about £ ¾ million has been expended in bringing Dublin's shipping facilities up to date. An energetic dredging policy has been followed, accommodation for large vessels has been greatly extended, while the other improvements effected include new wharves and sheds, graving slips, a new breakwater and lighthouse, and a 100-ton crane.'

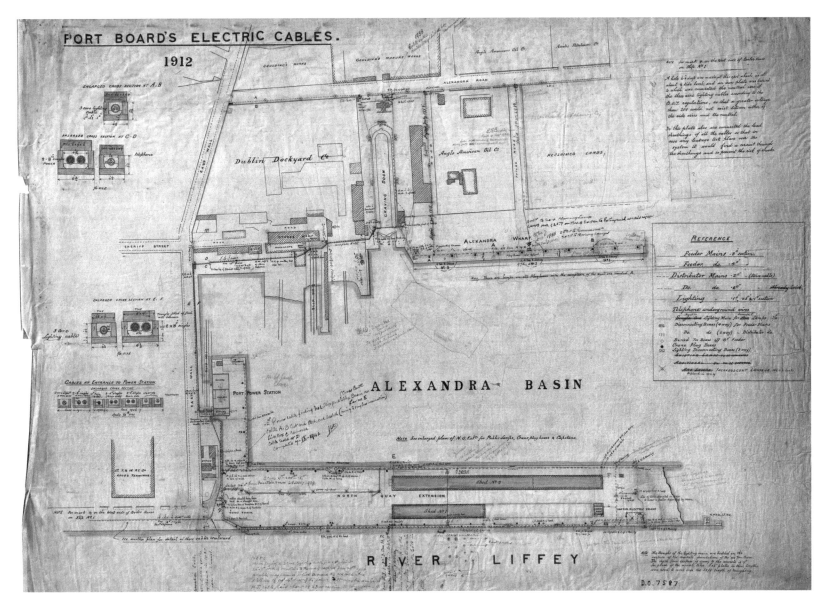

Above:

Schematic of Port Board's Electric Cables in 1912

Left:

Staff of Port Powerstation, c1912

Right:

Interior of Port Powerstation, commissioned 1907

100 tonne crane under construction and in use at Dublin Port

Shipbuilding and repair

In 1902, Purser Griffith had become a Director of the newly formed Dublin Dockyard Company, based at Alexandra Basin, North Wall. He had supported the development of the dockyard from its revival in 1901 by Smellie and Scott, two Clyde ship designers. Smellie met Purser Griffith on his second visit to Dublin Port and found him to be an enthusiastic advocate of the proposal to revive the shipbuilding and repairing activities in the port. Purser Griffith promised his support in all matters concerning the efficiency of the port and its equipment. The fitting out wharf at the entrance to the graving dock was reconstructed and the berth dredged. Operations began in December of 1901 and the first steamer, the Gertie, was launched on 4th October 1902. The dockyard was situated between the No.1 Graving Dock and the Patent Slips, part of the area now occupied by the Port Centre.

Although Dublin was never renowned as a centre for ship building, the industry had been carried out on a small scale from time to time from as early as the 17th century, and between 1902 and 1914, some sixty ships were built and launched and many others repaired. In 1915 Purser Griffith and the other two directors formed an associated company to manufacture shells, a factory being erected for the purpose within the shipyard premises.

In a paper to the ICEI in 1917, Purser Griffith's son, John William, remarked that it was common knowledge that his father had taken a good deal of trouble to bring the question of port revenue and proper administration before the public, so that something might be done to place the revenue of the port on a proper basis. In the ensuing discussion, Pierce Purcell said that he felt that engineers should have a considerable say in the policy by which undertakings were to be carried out and constructed. Then, possibly, they would have a little less talk and a great deal more solid work. He thought that engineers had been getting rather squeezed out from having much say on public bodies and public companies, 'they being looked upon as mere machines for carrying out work.

As early as 1901, Purser Griffith had written a memorandum for the Board on the subject of its financial policy and had provided all the facts and figures in support of his contention that the future well-being of the port would be jeopardised if the Board did not make adequate provision for a programme of continual improvements. As Purser Griffith remarked '... Dublin, from its geographical position and lines of communication, is the natural commercial gateway to the greater part of Ireland, and should be treated as a national, and not merely a local asset.'

A clause was inserted in the 1902 Port Act which restricted the financing of improvement works using borrowed money and, prevented the Board from using accumulated revenues for the purpose. By 1909, Purser Griffith had presented an up-dated report to the Board in which he voiced his opinion that, unless the Board obtained further borrowing powers from parliament, improvement works, other than those already scheduled, would have to be financed out of revenue. He felt that the Board needed a settled financial policy to enable it to borrow on the security of its property and other resources. By comparison with ports, such as Belfast and Glasgow, the debt at Dublin Port was relatively small and port charges and cost of maintenance low, thus Purser Griffith felt that there was no reason why the rates on goods entering the port could not be raised by 50% to improve revenue, whilst still being competitive. Nevertheless, with very limited resources and restricted borrowing powers, works of improvement of great advantage to the port were carried out by Purser Griffith during his time as Engineer-in-Chief.

He continued to urge the Board to use accumulated revenue reserves for port improvements, rather than further borrowing (this was then the generally accepted financial practice in the principal ports in the UK). He specifically proposed that the revenue raised be used to rebuild the Custom House Docks and adjacent quaysides, with the intention of bringing deep-water facilities closer to the city to relieve congestion at the North Wall. As we now know, this was not proceeded with and the port moved, instead, even further down river.

Amunition workers at
Dublin Dockland Company
c.1915.

Resignations

Frustrated at the Board's reluctance to build on what had been achieved in providing deep-water facilities, and being in total opposition to its financial policies, Purser Griffith decided in late 1912 that his only course of action was to seek early retirement and fight the Board from within. He considered that the Board representatives of the ship-owners formed a powerful lobby that was against further development. It seemed to him to be in their interests to have the large ocean-going vessels go elsewhere to unload and to have goods trans-shipped to Dublin in their own coastal vessels.

Purser Griffith's involvement in the commercial life of the city (e.g. his directorship of the Dublin Dockyard Company) qualified him to go forward for election to the Board as a trader's representative and he was duly elected to the Dublin Port & Docks Board in January 1915. Throughout the next eighteen months, his disagreement with policy developed into a major controversy and culminated in his resignation from the Board in July 1916.

His reasons for resigning was that he was entirely opposed to the policy of the special expenditure committee, which had been adopted by a majority of the Board. Nearly four months had been spent by the committee in various investigations, resulting in sundry recommendations, which as far as Purser Griffith could see, would not mitigate the financial stress of the Board, but in many ways were calculated to interfere with the economical and efficient management of the port. Purser Griffith stated that 'the chief aim (of the Board) seems to have been to divert attention from the real cause of the Board's financial embarrassment, and (to) try to throw the blame on the Board's officers. During a long and somewhat wide experience I have never met with a more discreditable procedure. The Board's difficulties are not due to excessive expenditure on works of improvement or maintenance, not to strikes or war conditions, but to a disregard to some of the elementary principles of public finance. It will be said that the Board are taking steps to set their house in order by raising the harbour rates and dues to their statutory maximum, but this should not have been necessary, and unless this is accompanied by a financial policy to curtail expenditure on interest, and to build up adequate reserves for the repayment of loans and the renewal of plant, machinery and works, I see no prospect of improvement.'

And so ended the Purser Griffith connection with Dublin Port, but not with his adopted city. On the day following his resignation in 1916 from the Dublin Port & Docks Board, his son, John William, tendered his resignation from the position of Engineer-in-Chief which, though couched in different terms from that of his father, was based on a similar conflict with the Board's policy of seeking to achieve economies in the costs of port maintenance and development by reductions in staff. John William Griffith had been Assistant Engineer on the construction of Rosslare Harbour before joining his father in 1903 as Assistant Engineer at Dublin Port.

Purser Griffith (second from right) with staff at Dublin Port in 1900

Purser Griffith's involvement in the commercial life of the city (e.g. his directorship of the Dublin Dockyard Company) qualified him to go forward for election to the Board as a trader's representative and he was duly elected to the Dublin Port & Docks Board in January 1915.

The eminent consultant

Above:
Openings of Scherzer twin rolling lift bridges over entrance to Royal Canal Harbour, installed 1912

Opposite page:
Scherzer rolling lift bridge over entrance to Royal Canal, 1912

Sir John P.Griffith & Partners

Both of Purser Griffith's sons, John William and Frederick Purser, joined their father in a small engineering consultancy practice established in 1917 as Sir John P.Griffith & Partners with offices at 6 Dame Street in the city. The offices were on the corner of Palace Street and Dame Street nearly opposite the Olympia Theatre and beside Mason's the Opticians and Ging's the Theatrical Outfitters, all demolished in recent years. John William's son Evan also joined the family firm, but was to die at the early age of 29.

The work of the office was never extensive, but became a base for the development of a number of projects of national importance, in particular the development of the country's water power and peat resources. Purser Griffith had become an experienced engineer and an authority on harbour engineering in particular. He had been consulted already by a number of harbour authorities whilst at Dublin Port. For instance, in 1895-6, he was retained by the Dundalk Harbour Commissioners to advise on what improvements should be made to the approaches to the port. He was critical of John Neville's report and designs of 1864, but did acknowledge that 'it is only just to bear in mind that the shipping requirements of his day were very different to present day requirements.'

His detailed printed report typifies his meticulous analysis of the marine engineering problems faced by many ports, such as those on the river Mersey at Liverpool and the river Humber at Hull, both of which benefited from Sir John's experience.

In 1920, Trinity College Dublin accepted an offer of assistance from Sir John to introduce aspects of harbour and other marine works into the curriculum of the engineering degree course. The decree of the University Council read as follows: *"Whereas it is expedient that eminent specialists should be brought into connection with the professional schools of the University, and whereas Sir John Purser Griffith, M.A.I.(h.c.) is greatly distinguished in the science and practice of Harbour Engineering.., he be appointed Honorary Professor of Harbour Engineering... to perform such duties as may from time to time be agreed on between him and the Board."* Sir John presented models to the Engineering School of some of the works which had been completed during his time at Dublin Port.

Purser Griffith had received an Honorary Master of Engineering (MAI) in 1914 from the University of Dublin and an Honorary Doctor of Science (DSc) from the National University of Ireland was conferred on him in 1938, a short while before his 90th birthday. He was elected a Member of the Royal Irish Academy on 15 March, 1919 and, with his marine engineering experience, served as a Commissioner of Irish Lights from 1913 to 1933.

Purser Griffith had earned his knighthood in 1911, not for his work at Dublin Port, but for representing Ireland on the Royal Commission appointed in March 1906 'to enquire into and to report on the canals and inland navigations of the United Kingdom.' The commission was asked to inquire into the condition and financial position of the canals and waterways of the UK, and the improvements and extensions desirable to complete a system of through communication by water between centres of commercial, industrial or agriculture importance, and between such centres and the sea.

One proposal was for the State to take over the canals. Purser Griffith asked William Field, M.P. for the St.Patrick's Division of Dublin and Chairman of the Industrial Development Association, whether he would consider individual members of all the county councils and boroughs in Ireland to be a suitable board of control. Field agreed with Purser Griffith and remarked that 'he had the greatest confidence in the administrative powers of my fellow-countrymen, and I do not care whether they are Orangemen or Freemasons so long as they are Irishmen!'

Reading through the lengthy Minutes of Evidence given to the Commission, one forms the distinct impression that Purser Griffith was particularly concerned with the effect of any recommendations on trade through Dublin Port – he was of course Engineer-in-Chief of the Port at the time and should have been considered to have had a vested interest. Nevertheless, he was considered to have served his King well and he was duly rewarded by him with a Knighthood at an investiture at St James's Palace in London in July 1911.

At one point in the enquiry, George Stevenson, a commissioner representing the Board of Works, was questioned by Purser Griffith on the state of the Royal Canal, which had been purchased by the Midland Great Western Railway in 1846 for around £300,000. The railway company maintained the navigation and charged tolls, but did not promote it and were not carriers. Purser Griffith expressed his opinion that the canal should be handed over to the OPW, an event which was, in fact, to happen some 70 years later. Purser Griffith also advocated the deepening and widening of the Grand and Royal canals and the rebuilding of the tidal locks at Dublin, in order to increase the volume of trade through the port. Again, when hearing the evidence of the Manager of the Grand Canal Co., Purser Griffith concentrated on affairs affecting the port.

Of some historical interest is Purser Griffith's visit, with other members of the Commission, to Kilkenny in September 1906. They met with representatives of the Kilkenny Industrial Development Association to hear their views on the proposed construction of a canal from Kilkenny to the tidal limit of the River Nore near Inistioge. The proposed still-water canal had been designed by the County Surveyor of Kilkenny, Alexander Burden. It was to be 35 feet wide at the water surface, 5 feet 6 inches deep and to parallel the Nore for some 19 ½ miles (Burden considered that it would not have been feasible to use the river channel for navigation). There were to be 18 locks, each 80 feet long by 16 feet wide with 5 feet depth over the sill. The original abortive attempt at constructing a navigation was commenced by Omer and Ockenden in 1755, but Purser Griffith found that virtually no traces of the canal had survived. The Commission recommended that the canal might be constructed with State aid and this suggestion probably sounded its death knell.

The final recommendations of the Royal Commission on Canals and Waterways were: the unification and improvement of certain waterways; the establishment of a Waterway Board for England and a Water Board for Ireland; a standard to be adopted for dimensions of improved waterways; and the transference of railway-owned waterways to the Waterway Board. Purser Griffith was later nominated by the Permanent Committee of the International Navigation Congress as General Reporter on the utilisation of waterways for the production of power, and presented his report in 1923.

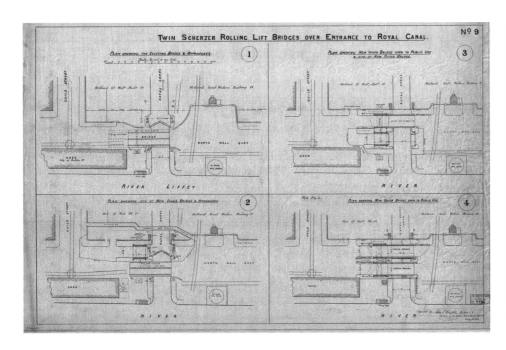

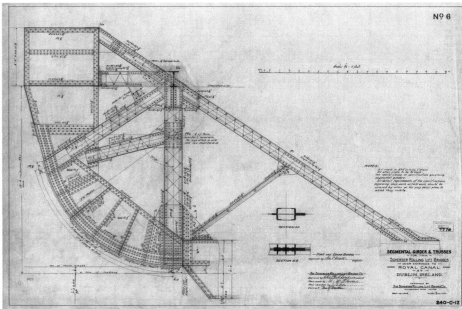

Engineering consultancies

The Board at Dublin Port were generous in allowing Purser Griffith a wider consulting role and he acted as Advising Engineer to the Government on Wicklow Harbour and the Foreshore Works at Arklow Harbour. In January 1907, Purser Griffith joined the Vice-Regal Commission appointed to consider the replacement of Lemuel Cox's timber trestle bridge over the River Suir at Waterford and was also a member of a similar commission which reported on the replacement of the bridge over the River Shannon at Portumna.

In August 1910, the Dublin City Surveyor & Waterworks Engineer, John G.O'Sullivan, asked Purser Griffith for advice on the sinking of the puddle trench at the additional storage reservoir at Roundwood. Again, in November of the following year, Purser Griffith was asked to inspect the new works at Roundwood, in particular with regard to the nature of the rock in the puddle trench and to furnish a report. He commanded a fee of £15 per day, a not inconsiderable sum in those days, and a reflection of Purser Griffith's standing as a consultant.

His consultancy practice was responsible in 1925 for the design of the present Annesley Bridge over the river Tolka, a three-span concrete and steel structure which replaced an earlier masonry arch bridge erected in 1796/7. Site investigation revealed rock at depths of 54-61 feet and the new abutments and piers rest on concrete piles driven down to the rock. The contractors were Orr, Watt & Co. of Motherwell, who were able to outbid five Irish contractors for the contract.

In the same year, Sir John and Sir Maurice Fitzmaurice were consulted by the British government on proposals to construct a Barrage and Tidal Power Station in the River Severn Estuary. An observer in the Irish Builder & Engineer commented 'Irish engineers, whose 'amour pro-pre' (self esteem) has latterly been stung severely (a reference to German engineers and the Shannon Scheme) can apply the emollient that the talent and experience of one of the recognised leaders of the profession in this country (Purser Griffith) has been welcomed elsewhere.'

A commentator at the time remarked 'It is, we believe, the first time in its *(the Institution of Civil Engineers)* history that this great honour has been conferred upon an Irish engineer whose practice has been in his own country. It is also a compliment to Ireland, one which, we feel sure, not alone Irish engineers, but all Irishmen, especially those associated with engineers in the cognate professions and callings, will feel proud of.'

The Institution of Civil Engineers

Purser Griffith was elected an Associate Member of the Institution of Civil Engineers (ICE) in 1877 and in 1879, at the age of 31, delivered his important paper on 'Improvements of the Bar of Dublin by Artificial Scour', for which he was received a Manby Premium. His paper gave rise to much debate about the best ways of adapting the natural regimes of harbours and estuaries to provide deeper approach channels for shipping. Purser Griffith was a member of the Council of the ICE from 1910, Vice-President in 1916 and President for the session 1918-19. During his presidency, he presented the large crystal chandeliers and the painted central roof panel in the Great Hall at Great George Street in London, the panel, executed by Charles Sims, R.A., forming a memorial to those members who had given their lives in WW1.

In his presidential address in 1919, Purser Griffith considered his election as 'the greatest honour an engineer can receive.' He said that he had hesitated to allow his name to go forward on account of his age (he was then 71) and the distance of his residence from London (Dublin), but concluded that it would have been 'ungracious to decline the great honour' and recognised his 'responsibility to Wales, my native land, and to Ireland, the land of my adoption, which I have represented on the Council for so many years, and where the whole of my professional life has been spent.' He accepted the position 'as an honour conferred on Ireland which, with all her faults and failings, grows dearer to you the longer you live there.'

Purser Griffith took over the presidency at a time when the Great War had just ended and the world was looking forward to peaceful progress. The ICE had just marked the centenary of its foundation. An issue at the time was the desirability or otherwise of forming local associations, another being that of the registration of engineers. Membership at the time stood at about 9,000 and there were active student associations in a number of large centres of population outside London.

Purser Griffith felt that two questions of importance had recently come before the ICE Council. The first, that the ICE was not sufficiently in touch with the members, and he advocated strongly the formation of local associations or federated societies in preference to institutions operating completely independently. On the second question of the registration of engineers, 97% of replies from a survey of members around 1919 affirmed that membership should be 'an undoubted proof of the highest qualifications.' In 1886, the ICE had expressly discountenanced the use of the letters 'CE' as not founded on any qualification and as calculated to mislead.

Purser Griffith, referring to his 1916 James Forrest Lecture on economic problems in connection with the handling of raw materials and merchandise at ports and other large centres of traffic, made a plea for the equipping of ports, and endeavoured to show that the old term 'labour-saving appliances' should be replaced by that of 'labour-aiding appliances', because he maintained that the aim should be greater productivity and not a reduction in the labour force. He regretted the end of industries where the master worked alongside his workers. This was due largely to the introduction of limited liability companies with boards of management and the formation of trade unions. It appeared to him that the only remedy was the widespread adoption of co-operation, co-partnership, and profit-sharing, thus ensuring that the workers participated fully in the prosperity of the industries in which they were engaged. In this view he was somewhat ahead of his time.

In conclusion, Purser Griffith felt that he was expected to make some reference to what the engineering profession had done in Ireland. He began by saying that 'The story of engineering achievements in that delightful land is one of the brightest spots in its sad history. If religious intolerance and political trickery and intrigue could be banished, and the land handed over to the guidance and control of engineers, what prospects would be opened up of industrial progress and contentment'. Although an extreme and rather naïve view of Irish society, he no doubt felt strongly that the engineering profession should play a much larger part in the affairs of state.

Development of natural resources

Peat development

Following the end of WW1, Purser Griffith, in his presidential address to the 'Civils' in London, noted that economy was the cry of the day, but stressed that it was false economy for a nation to reduce expenditure by not developing its resources. He went on to point to the short-sightedness of letting the inland waterways become derelict and allowing agricultural land to go out of cultivation. It was also false economy to allow the peat bogs to remain undrained and unreclaimed, when they might become a source of national wealth in food and fuel. He felt that coal reserves would eventually run out and that water-power resources should be developed. The development of our peat and water-power resources was an urgent and pressing need, but he considered that neither could be progressed without state intervention.

Meanwhile in Dublin, P.H.McCarthy, in his presidential address to the ICEI in November 1919, when speaking on "reconstruction", noted that the scarcity of materials, the enormous increase in taxation, and the high cost of labour, all stood in the way of enterprise and development. He referred to the valuable paper by Chaloner Smith on the flow of the river Shannon at Killaloe and he hoped that the government committee on water power in Ireland would obtain information about all Irish rivers. 'The utilisation of water-power should be approached from a scientific and business point of view." McCarthy considered that Purser Griffith's election as president of the 'Civils' had been "a tribute to his brilliant achievements and to the interest he had taken in the profession.'

The long and fascinating history of the winning of turf by both hand and mechanised methods has been ably recounted by Feehan and O'Donovan in their treatise on the Bogs of Ireland. Mechanised methods of winning peat did not happen suddenly with the advent of Bord na Mona, but can be traced back to the middle of the last century. Peat or turf was used as a fuel for both domestic and industrial purposes, in particular in the smelting of iron and steel and raising steam to drive both stationary and locomotive engines. Charles Wye Williams (1844) and Charles Hodgson (1860) made determined efforts to produce briquettes by the artificial drying and consolidation of peat, the latter entrepreneur being credited with the invention of the peat briquette press. Other than the limitations of the technology and the considerable maintenance, the main problem faced by these early enterprises was that coal could be delivered to Dublin at a lower price than that of the peat briquettes, and thus promising enterprises were technically sound but economically not feasible, at least not without State subventions.

In 1907-8, Professor Hugh Ryan, professor of chemistry at UCD (1899 – 1931), summarised earlier attempts to harvest and process peat in Ireland, and reviewed the existing state of peat technology. He also translated the 'bible' of German peat producers. The coal panic of the war years had drawn attention to the unused peat deposits in the UK, and in 1917 the Director of Fuel Research, Sir George Beilby, and the Fuel Research Board, decided to set up a small committee of inquiry into the utilisation of Irish peat deposits. Purser Griffith was Chairman of this committee, Pierce Purcell Secretary, and it also included Hugh Ryan.

The Irish Peat Enquiry Committee devoted much time and thought to the subject and came to the conclusion that the reclamation of the bogs for agricultural purposes could be successfully combined with the winning of peat for fuel, but that the introduction of mechanical winning and handling was essential. The reports of the committee, dated February 1918 and July 1918, together with the reports upon them by the Fuel Research Board, were in the hands of the Westminster government by September 1918, but they were pigeon-holed and nothing further was heard of them. The British Government, and similarly the Irish Free State Government, failed to act on the recommendations of a later 1921-22 Committee.

'Civilisation on its physical side is based on fuel.' With this sweeping statement, Sir George Beilby, FRS, Director of Fuel Research, opened the James Forrest Lecture delivered to the Institution of Civil Engineers in London in 1921. The experience of the war years had brought home to people the value of a regular and unlimited supply of fuel and, to those who had given thought to the question, the problem of increasing the supply of native fuel in Ireland appeared one of the most urgent to be dealt with by the government. In 1921, coal imports were running at around 4.5 million tons per annum, whereas coal mined in Ireland was only 100,000 tons, but some 6-7 million tons of air-dried peat was used. In terms of heat units, it was reckoned that imported coal accounted for 55% of our heat requirements.

In speaking about the reconstruction and industrial development of Ireland, Pierce Purcell said '...it has usually been regarded as the outward and visible signs of patriotism to speak in an extravagant way as to the value of our resources. To exaggerate our resources in fuel and water-power is one of the worst possible services to the community, but, on the other hand, nothing can be more mischievous than to take up the attitude that this country is entirely agricultural, and will always remain so.'

Irish Peat Enquiry Committee at Turraun about 1920 (Griffith second from right)

The Irish Peat Enquiry Committee devoted much time and thought to the subject and came to the conclusion that the reclamation of the bogs for agricultural purposes could be successfully combined with the winning of peat for fuel, but that the introduction of mechanical winning and handling was essential.

Reviewing the whole position (on peat fuel), Purcell considered that 'there is a future for peat fuel in this country. It will take considerable working up, but if success is attained, the result will well repay the efforts employed. Our climate has had many hard things said about it, but I am not at all convinced that it is less suited for a successful peat industry than that of any peat-consuming country that I am aware of.'

Frustrated at the inertia of successive governments and the seeming total lack of appreciation of the value of Ireland's natural resources. Purser Griffith decided to mount a personal campaign to show what could be done. The ultimate development of the bogs owes a great deal to his early work and inspiration. He spent around £70,000 of his inherited fortune to show, by example, what could be done. Purser Griffith purchased bogs at Ticknevin near Edenderry and at Turraun near Ballycumber, where in 1924 he set up the Leinster Carbonising Company Limited. Here, at the age of 76, he established one of the earliest machine peat operations in Ireland, using German machinery adapted to suit local conditions. Sir John's objective in setting up the works at Turraun was to show on a small scale what he knew could be achieved on a much larger scale, provided there was sufficient government investment. Purser Griffith was fond of using a quotation from James Fintan Lawlor: "Somewhere, and somehow, and by somebody, a beginning must be made."

In a paper presented to the ICEI in 1933, Purser Griffith dealt extensively with the question of peat and its economic importance to Ireland. The Minister for Industry & Commerce, Sean Lemass, associating himself with the vote of thanks to Purser Griffith, noted that the paper 'laid stress on the indifference and ignorance that had been found to exist surrounding the possibilities and potentialities of the bogs of Ireland. If there were indifference and ignorance, the blame for it could in no way be laid at Sir John's door, because there was probably no man – certainly very few – who had worked so consistently as he in order to remove both'. However, Lemass went on to say that he 'was not convinced that the utilisation of machinery for the winning of peat had any very great advantage over the method which had been in use in Ireland for a very large number of years; that was the ordinary method of winning peat by hand.' The year following saw the establishment of the Turf Development Board and the taking over by the state of Purser Griffith's Turraun Works. Pierce Purcell remarked that he had first met Sir John in 1917 when the Irish Peat Inquiry was carrying out its work. He said that 'No committee appointed by the state had laboured so zealously or honestly as than committee, which acted under the guidance of Sir John. Sir John had over many years contributed much useful knowledge and assistance towards the development of peat, and the country was under a great debt of obligation to him for all that he had accomplished. He had carried out work which really should have been undertaken by the state.'

Water power

Shortages caused by WW1 had given a boost to those who sought alternatives to the use of imported coal. In particular, attention was directed to the utilisation of water power for the generation of electricity. In June 1918, the President of the Board of Trade, with the concurrence of the Minister of Reconstruction, appointed a committee, under the Chairmanship of Sir John Snell, to examine and report upon the water-power resources of the UK, and the extent to which they could be made available for industrial purposes. In August of the same year, it was decided to appoint a sub-committee to deal specifically with Ireland, with Purser Griffith as Chairman. He had for some time been critical of the failure of the administration and Irish industrialists for not making use of natural resources.

The formation of the Water Power Resources Committee in 1918 was due to the representations of Laurence J. Kettle, the Dublin City Electrical Engineer and Manager, a position he held until the Dublin Corporation Electricity Department was taken over by the ESB in 1929. He remained as an adviser to the ESB and in 1934 became a member of the Board. There was already a mass of information in the reports of the Board of Works and the committee had access to them, in particular to the surveys and calculations of John Chaloner Smith. There were a great number of sources of power on the principal rivers to be examined, but in all cases there were conflicts of interest to be dealt with, such as navigation, drainage, fishing, and existing milling rights. It was felt generally that there was little hope of dealing thoroughly and economically with such problems unless they could be coordinated under some unified state control, which could deal with them upon broad lines of national utility. The committee reported in May 1921. Another commission of enquiry, set up by the Sinn Féin government under the chairmanship of Hugh Ryan, came to broadly the same conclusion and reported in January 1922 in favour of the greater use of the country's water resources for the generation of electricity.

Both committees found that considerable water powers were available and that economic development was possible. The committees did not agree as to the amount of power available, but the fact remained that a clear prima facie case had been established for developing a number of sites. Purcell considered that it should have been possible to have the technical and financial aspects of two of the most promising schemes investigated in detail by an independent technical commission and, on receipt of a favourable report, the government might partially finance the schemes. Whilst he was opposed to the nationalisation of industry, transport and mining services, on general grounds, he thought that the state should assume some responsibility for the initial steps in setting up and developing hitherto undeveloped or partially developed industries, i.e. pump priming the efforts of Irish entrepreneurs, such as Purser Griffith.

Purser Griffith noted that 'with the advances made in electrical transmission, I look forward hopefully to a linking up of the scattered water resources in Ireland into a useful service to supplement our fuel resources.' He concluded his presidential address to the ICE in 1919 with these words – 'I may be told that I am old man who dreams. I admit it; but the dreams I dream, and like to dream, are those which recall the magnificent work done by our profession in the past...', but he was confident that the engineering profession would be to the forefront in any future development of Ireland.

George Marshall Harriss, who was General Manager of the Dublin United Tramway Company, was strongly in favour of developing the application of electrical power. He noted that industry was 'dependent on a reliable source of cheap energy and electricity was seen as the most suitable and flexible form of energy' for that purpose. Harriss suggested a major coal-burning power station with a transmission network radiating outwards into which the small hydro-stations could feed. This, he felt, would maximise the use of the hydro-power potential of the rivers. When discussing the potential of the Liffey, he drew attention to the need to provide a large storage reservoir upstream of Poulaphuca. His paper, delivered on 2nd February 1920, attracted considerable discussion.

Surprisingly, Purser Griffith took no part in the discussion, but he was probably over in London attending to his presidential duties at the Civils. Like Purser Griffith, Harriss felt that other rivers, such as the Shannon, were not as attractive as the Liffey due to their distance from the perceived demand. J.M.Fay, referring to the possible development of the Erne, noted that transmission of electricity by cable had become so efficient that distance of consumer from source of supply should no longer be a problem.

James Read reminded those present that 'the larger the unit, the cheaper the service.' Chaloner Smith said he wished to see small general-utility power stations operating locally. He, like most commentators at the time, did not have the later vision of McLaughlin. Other speakers, such as Professor Seymour, concurred and discounted the idea of one major scheme on account of the necessity of flooding agricultural land. The president, PH.McCarthy, came down in favour of small schemes and estimated that the cost of land acquisition would swamp any scheme proposed for Poulaphuca. Some years previously, a scheme had been proposed to develop the power of the Shannon at Killaloe with additional storage at Lough Allen.

Following the establishment in 1921 of Saorstat Éireann, the Lord Lieutenant, Viscount Fitzalan, nominated Sir John to the Seanad and he served as a Senator from 1922 until his retirement in 1936, having been re-elected in 1932. Prior to the presentation of a paper by Michael Hogan (later to become Professor of Civil Engineering at UCD) at a meeting of the ICEI in 1924, the President, Pierce Purcell, expressed his pleasure at the earlier election of Purser Griffith to the Seanad, and said that they were all quite sure that Sir John would render very valuable service to the country in that position. In fact, we can be grateful for his vigilance in one particular respect. When the Jury Service Bill was placed before the Seanad in 1927, he realised that engineers had been excluded from the list of professionals to be exempted. His amendment was carried and engineers were added to the list.

Following Sir John's retirement from the Seanad in 1936, the Council of the Engineers' Association decided to apply for registration as a nominating body. It was reported that members of the 'Cumann' were taking very considerable interest in the proceedings of the Seanad and were obviously conscious of the lack of representation of the engineering profession following Sir John's retirement.

Hogan had been one of Purcell's students in UCD and was, at the time of his paper, Technical Officer of the River Gauging and Tidal Currents Committee of the Department of Scientific and Industrial Research in London. He had studied the question of hydrometric surveying in Switzerland, Germany, France and other countries, and had carried out much hydrometric work. He considered that there was an urgent need for a hydrometric survey in Ireland. He discussed the possibility of correlating catchment rainfall readings and evaporation assumptions with river flow, but this was a complex research problem. He felt that it was preferable to gauge directly using current meters. He considered that all questions of a water power survey should be left for a few years until sufficient stream flow records had been collected, rather than deriving flows from run-off calculated from rainfall. It was realised that the water power of a flat river, such as the Shannon, could be developed without storage, but that the Liffey, being a relatively short, steep river, required a large storage reservoir to be created. Marshall Harriss felt that sufficient information was available in existing records to allow the development of Irish water power resources for electricity generation purposes to proceed without further delay.

Frederick Griffith pointed out that the Water Power Commission, of which his father had been chairman, undoubtedly proved that it was possible to obtain, in a comparatively short time, a large quantity of power from the Liffey and that, in his opinion 'they could not afford to wait for 35 years (the period of useful rainfall data) to prove that they could do it.' He considered that 'it was pretty clear from the meteorological records that they had sufficient power at Poulaphuca to replace eight stations in Dublin' and that "they should get on with the work and not worry about very accurate details.' Much was made of the idea of harnessing the smaller water powers by linking them up with steam power stations, a similar concept to that of small hydro plants feeding into the national grid.

Purser Griffith, commenting on Hogan's recommendation that all question of a water power survey be postponed until a few years of stream flow records had been collected, wrote 'To postpone hydroelectric development in Ireland until such experimental work was carried out would mean the postponement of the utilisation of one of Ireland's most promising sources of power.' The most urgent need was unity of control of water for purposes in Ireland. Commission after commission had pressed for this. There was always conflict between the interests of navigation, drainage, water-power and fisheries.

Purser Griffith ended his written submission by congratulating the ICEI on the interest shown by its members in the development of Ireland's natural resources. That attitude inspired him with hope for the country's future. He believed that depended more on the engineer than the politician, and on the substitution of a constructive policy in place of the present destructive madness (January 1923) and may be summarised in the sentiment – "Work, not Talk."

Purser Griffith became a strong advocate of the development of the hydro-power potential of the Liffey and produced numerous pamphlets and articles on the subject. A private company, the Anna Liffey Power Development Co., Ltd., was established in 1923, with Sir John as its chairman, the other directors being Marshall Harriss, Alfred Delap, Darrel Figgis, Henry Homan Jeffcott and John William Griffith. Dublin Corporation had also become interested in the development of the Liffey and hired a Swiss consultant (Herr Buchi) to report on Purser Griffith's and other proposals and, in May 1922, he had recommended that such a scheme should be proceeded with.

Buchi's outline proposals were similar to those that been put forward by Purser Griffith, i.e. the construction of a 100 foot high masonry dam at Pollaphuca to create a large storage reservoir and a 12MW hydro-power station at Ballymore Eustace, with a smaller station at Leixslip. Peak load demand would be assisted by the steam plant at the existing Pigeon House station in Dublin. Sir John hoped that the Liffey scheme would be adopted as a national programme, something which had been expressed in the Water Power Resources of Ireland sub-committee report. However, his hopes were dashed by the continuing unrest and political uncertainty, which culminated in the Civil War. This was the principal reason why Sir John set up his own company to undertake the scheme. He engaged an independent expert, Dr Theodor Stevens, to examine his proposals which were costed at £1.2 million.

Purser Griffith became a strong advocate of the development of the hydro-power potential of the Liffey and produced numerous pamphlets and articles on the subject.

The Shannon Scheme;
working on the penstocks.
Source: ESB Archives
Photographic Collection.

The Shannon Scheme

I t was against the post-Civil War background, as the new government sought to translate its independence into the reality of social and economic progress, that the suggestion of a national electrification scheme was first made seriously. The idea of the Shannon Scheme was sold to the government by a young Irish engineer, Thomas McLaughlin.

He had been working with the German firm of Siemens-Schuckert in Berlin and, whilst there in the hydro-power design department, had developed a scheme for a one-step harnessing of the river Shannon at Ardnacrusha to produce electricity and distribute it nation-wide. He contacted Patrick McGilligan, whom he had known in his student days at UCD, and who had recently been elected to Dáil Éireann, and obtained his enthusiastic support for the scheme. Following the publication of a White Paper in March 1924, Siemens were asked to develop the proposals in more detail and these were examined by four expert assessors appointed by the government, their main findings being reported to the Dail on 19th December 1924. They endorsed the Siemens proposals and favoured McLaughlin's idea of harnessing the Shannon at Ardnacrusha. They felt that the Liffey could be developed at a later stage depending on how demand for electricity developed.

Having spent so much time and effort on advocating the Liffey Scheme, Sir John was naturally considerably displeased when the Free State government decided to proceed instead with the development of the power potential of the river Shannon. When the Shannon Scheme was first proposed, a commentator writing in the Irish Builder pointed out that 'many authorities of unquestionable technical ability, experience, and integrity, believed that it was too big for the country, as an initial experiment; that a start might have been made with a small scheme, such as the Liffey or Pollaphuca Scheme, and the results studied.'

However, the experts adjudged the Liffey scheme to be too small, that it would only supply Dublin, and that 80% of the State would not therefore be able to share in the advantages of an electricity supply. In the Dáil, minister McGilligan dismissed any possibility of the Liffey Scheme going ahead. Darrell Figgis, a member of the Dáil, had invested his life savings in Purser Griffith's Liffey scheme and he and Purser Griffith, who since 1922 had been a member of the Seanad, tried their best to rally public opinion in support of their scheme. The full report of the government experts was submitted to both houses of the Oireachtas on 7th January 1925 and just two weeks later McGilligan announced publicly that the government intended going ahead with the Shannon Scheme and that, from now on, he was 'paying no attention to uninformed critics.'

The Irish Builder & Engineer commented: 'The profession of engineering in the Free State appears to have been at first stunned to silence by either the scope of the scheme, or by such details as are at present comprehensible. On the other hand, the facts must not be overlooked that the Germans, as a race, are longheaded and practical in business, and that their engineers are amongst the best trained and most efficient in the world. Such men are quite unlikely 'to buy a pig on a poke'. The report was the real starting point for the controversy, which saw most of the leading members of the engineering profession in Ireland, including senior members of the ICEI, supporting Purser Griffith's views on the development of the country's water power resources.

The ICEI, In a letter to the Minister for Industry & Commerce dated 24th March 1924, gave a general welcome for the Government's intention to develop the water resources of the Free State, but the Council voiced grave concerns over the manner in which the contract was to given to Siemens-Schuckert without any independent assessment by experts or the application of normal procedures for open tendering on a scheme drawn up by consulting engineers. It was felt that the procedures proposed to be adopted were directly at variance with accepted principles of engineering practice. They feared that one contractor would be allowed a virtual monopoly in the supply of electricity to the country.

The Minister's lengthy reply was a model of political speak, but did make clear the government's intention of promoting the scheme itself, either as a state measure or by a public statutory body established under and controlled by the laws of the Free State. The Electricity Bill of 1926 did just that with the establishment of the Electricity Supply Board (ESB). Also a panel of experts was hired to advise the Government on the scheme before any contract was signed.

In January and April 1925, Purser Griffith published pamphlets, in which he set out the reasons why he could not support the government decision on the Shannon Scheme as:

1. Because I believe that by handing over the electrification of the Irish Free State to one firm of contractors the government are depriving the country of the freedom of contract which would allow of obtaining the best hydro-electric appliances which the world can produce and of obtaining the advantage of worldwide experience.

2. Because there is no possible reason for limiting the market to Germany: - the United States of America, Canada, Switzerland, and France have all greater experience of work such as is wanted in Ireland than Germany has.

3. Because the river Shannon presents the greatest difficulties of any river in Ireland in dealing with this problem in consequence of the conflicting interests of drainage, navigation, fishing and power.

4. Because in carrying out such a great experiment as the introduction of hydroelectric development in Ireland on a large scale, it is a recognised principle in scientific research to select the most favourable case for first consideration, investigation, and development.

5. Because this course helps to clear up the problem and simplify the issue. The real value of the hydro-electric installation will be discovered clear of secondary issues. The electric current will be generated at a clear and definite cost, without having to adjust it for damage to agricultural and other interests.

6. It is for this reason I favour the development of the water power resources of the Liffey, as a first stage of the general development throughout Ireland. This course is supported on the following grounds:

   (a) The demand for electric energy exists in the Dublin district.

   (b) An ample supply of water is available for the demand.

   (c) Facility exists for development and extension as the demand increases.

   (d) In the initial stages of the supply it would be possible to limit the capital expenditure so that the price of current, even in the early stages, would be reasonable.

7. No objection can be raised on the grounds that the firm of Siemens-Schuckert is unable to carry out the electrical portion of the work in a first class manner, but this does not remove the objection to the restriction of this portion of the work to one firm.

8. I do, however, most emphatically disapprove of the general design of the structural works.

9. In my opinion, they are ill-considered ineffective and dangerous:- They involve the State in

   (a) Engineering risks

   (b) Agricultural risks

   (c) Financial risks which cannot be justified.

10. There is a consensus of opinion as to the need for a complete system of drainage in the Shannon catchment basin. In my opinion it is of primary importance, and the order of works on this river should be:-

    (a) Drainage works

    (b) Power development

    (c) Fisheries and Navigation (105)

Right:
The Shannon Scheme; Luffelbagger, wagon train and group of figures, painting by Seán Keating.
Source: ESB Art Portfolio Catalogue

Far right:
The Shannon Scheme; Building-site with Luffelbagger and wagon train, painting by Seán Keating.
Source: ESB Art Portfolio Catalogue

Purser Griffith was now in full pursuit and in the Seanad on 31st March he demanded a new enquiry.

'While it is a matter of common knowledge that Sir John is closely identified with a hydro-electric development scheme nearer home (the Liffey Scheme), his patriotism, business capacity, technical experience, and integrity are equally well-known, not only in the Irish Free State, but by his professional colleagues throughout Europe.' It was therefore not possible to simply dismiss his views, and it was felt that his notes 'deserved careful consideration as they were not written in a spirit of hot hostility, but (were) a careful analysis of methods than of technicalities, with the corollary, perhaps, that such methods would be unnecessary were the scheme technically sound.'

In spite of this, McGilligan was determined to see the Shannon Scheme become a reality and on 1st May the Shannon Electricity Bill was introduced in the Dáil. The writer in the Irish Builder & Engineer had concluded by saying that, provided the scheme was carried out for a fixed sum contract, then other arguments carried less weight. There the debate appeared to end and everyone wished the scheme well, including Purser Griffith, who generously turned over all his reports and data to the state.

By August a contract was signed between the government and Siemens-Schuckert to undertake the Shannon Scheme for the sum of £5.2 million and a completion time of 3½ years. The Ardnacrusha Power Station was officially opened by Prime Minister William T.Cosgrave on the 22nd July 1929, less than six years since McLaughlin first approached the government with his proposals, a truly remarkable achievement, which led a commentator in England to refer to the Shannon Scheme as the 'eighth wonder of the world'.

Dublin Port Chief Engineers
John Purser Griffith (1848-1938)

Purser Griffith, in an introductory note to a pamphlet written by his son, John William Griffith and Professor Jeffcott, published in 1921, recounted that he had been intimately acquainted with the river Liffey for over half a century, and with its vagaries in times of flood and drought. When he became Chairman of the Sub-Committee appointed by the Board of Trade to investigate the Water Power Resources of Ireland, he had come to realise just how important an industrial and commercial asset the river was for the city and surrounding district. The river had been used for power purposes for centuries before and there were still some industries along its banks partly worked by water power, mostly flour mills.

The variable flow of Irish rivers was the principal reason why the use of water power on a large scale had been restricted. The only remedy was the provision of large storage reservoirs. However, as long as there was access to cheap imported coal, steam plant provided the most reliable and cheapest source of power. When the price of coal escalated, the government was forced to investigate the water power resources of the country. The whole problem of utilising the Liffey for power purposes turned on the provision of ample storage and the physical features of the upper basin of the river were found to be especially favourable for this purpose.

Purser Griffith found that there was more than sufficient water power to produce electricity in excess of that being provided at the time by seven different generating stations in the Dublin area [These were Dublin Corporation, Dublin United Tramways Co., Pembroke Urban District Council, Rathmines Urban District Council, Dublin Port & Docks Board, Great Northern Railway of Ireland (Sutton to Amiens Street), and the Dublin & Lucan Electric Railway Co.]

John William Griffith, working with his father, carried out the detailed surveys and published a description of the water power resources of the Liffey from source to sea. His paper included an accurate determination, from rainfall and flow records, of the power available. A masonry dam at Poulaphuca (later built in mass concrete) would raise the water level to a maximum of 600 feet O.D., thus creating a reservoir 3,874 acres in extent with a storage capacity of over 3 million cubic feet. He reckoned that 39 million units of electricity would be available to Dublin at ¾ pence per unit.

'In the proposed scheme for the development of the water power resources of the Liffey they looked forward to the formation of a beautiful lake in the basin of the Upper Liffey and King's River, which, if connected with Dublin by an efficient electric train service, would make that area a delightful resort for the citizens'. Following investigations in 1934-5, the Department of Industry & Commerce on balance advised against proceeding with the scheme, but were overruled by the Executive Council. It was obviously more economical to construct a combined hydro-electric and water supply scheme and the ESB and Dublin Corporation reached agreement on a sharing of the water storage to be provided by the reservoir near Blessington. At this stage, Purser Griffith generously made all his data and calculations available to the authorities.

In October 1937 an order was placed for the main construction work at Pollaphuca and Golden Falls and construction commenced in 1938. Purser Griffith was not to see the completion of the scheme as he died that year and, in any event, WW2 intervened and delayed construction, due mainly to a shortage of materials. The scheme was not completed until 1945, although it had been found possible to commission the smaller unit at Golden Falls by the temporary by-passing of the dam under construction at Pollaphuca.

Transatlantic terminus

Another of Purser Griffith's visionary proposals was to create a major national transatlantic terminal port in Galway Bay with an associated international airport at Oranmore. This idea was first mooted in 1919, but it was in the late 1920s, in the face of a threatened stoppage of the American mails and passengers from landing in or departing from Ireland, that the proposals began to take shape, aided by his son John William Griffith. The speed and size of the transatlantic liners had increased to the point where the saving of time by sending the mails through Queenstown (Cobh) instead of Liverpool had become insignificant. In any event, the largest and fastest liners had by then begun to transfer from Liverpool to Southampton.

Purser Griffith was influenced in his thinking by the words of Viscount Morley, some forty years previously when he was Chief Secretary for Ireland, who urged 'Do not let Ireland be pushed off the great high road between the West and the East.' In the autumn of 1928, Purser Griffith was able to get the Seanad to pass unanimously a resolution demanding that the development of Galway as a national harbour should be investigated.

To make it attractive for the steamship companies, such as Cunard and White Star, Purser Griffith considered that it would be necessary to provide a port into which the largest and fastest vessels could enter at all states of the tide. He was no doubt using the experience gained earlier at Dublin and elsewhere to deal with the technical problems involved. These, in fact, were few as the natural harbour of Galway Bay and the proximity of deep water to the coastline west of Galway city presented an ideal location, as he saw it, for a great national port. He claimed a number of advantages for the scheme, such as a saving of 1,050 miles in the crossing of the Atlantic (Halifax, Nova Scotia - Galway as against New York - Southampton) and felt that Galway won out over other west coast locations and, indeed, would be a much better proposition than the further development of Cork harbour. There had been earlier proposals with regard to Galway Bay, namely in 1852, 1913 and again in 1917. Galway Harbour Commissioners were also concerned about the limited facilities that they offered shipping companies. The only wet dock was frequently subject to silting and was not capable of accommodating liner tenders at all states of the tide. The North German Lloyd Line had found this out to their cost during the period that their liners from Halifax called at Galway. They did however, land some 4,000 tourists and they, for the most part, seemed to have been charmed by the reception they received at the hands of the Galwegians and there was only praise for the facilities provided.

The site selected by Purser Griffith was at Furbough, about six miles west of Galway city, between Barna and Spiddal (In 1917 the government had plans for spending no less than £7 million on a naval port at the site to trans-ship men and materials from Canada in support of the allied war effort).

Purser Griffith's plan was simple enough, provided funding could be made available. It envisaged the building of a long shelter breakwater and a number of deep-water jetties projecting from the shore. These facilities were to be connected to the national rail network at Galway. His associated idea was to develop Oranmore into an international airport to convey passengers and baggage onwards to Britain and continental destinations and in this he was supported by Arthur Cox, a director of Irish Airways Ltd., who was trying to start up a civil aviation service between Ireland and Britain. It was even suggested that passengers could be issued with free onward air tickets as an incentive to disembark from their Atlantic crossing at Galway!

Needless to say, the proposals invoked a sharp, but somewhat tardy, response from the Cork lobby, in the form of John Horgan, a former chairman of the Cork Harbour Commissioners. His article in Studies, under the title 'Irish Ports and Common Sense', was published some two years after Purser Griffith's article, and opened with the statement that 'The western and southern coasts of Ireland are dotted with ports which only exist in the lively imaginations of civil engineers.' Horgan continued – 'Engineers, in dealing with this question, invariably put the cart before the horse. Once they have found a place which is physically suitable for a port, or which by the expenditure of a few million pounds can be made so, they consider the problem to be solved and do not consider the more serious question as to whether it will be used after it is constructed.'

He considered that Cork harbour provided an infinitely better anchorage and safe approach than Southampton and the harbour commissioners had offered to provide an extension to the existing deep-water quay at Cobh, but the steamship companies were not interested. He felt that expenditure on such schemes as those put forward by engineers such as Purser Griffith would be of no national or local benefit other than the employment involved in their construction. As things turned out, advances in aviation technology led to the adoption of Foynes as a transatlantic flying boat base, and subsequently to the development of an international airport on the north bank of the Shannon estuary. These events finally dampened any further enthusiasm for Galway as a transatlantic passenger terminal.

To make it attractive for the steamship companies, such as Cunard and White Star, Purser Griffith considered that it would be necessary to provide a port into which the largest and fastest vessels could enter at all states of the tide. He was no doubt using the experience gained earlier at Dublin and elsewhere to deal with the technical problems involved.

Churchman and benefactor

The Moravian Church

All his life Purser Griffith had been very loyal to his Moravian faith and supported the Moravian Church in both its home and foreign activities. He was a member of the congregation of the Dublin Moravian Church in Bishop Street. Purser Griffith always sought to direct his gifts so as to encourage others to help as well, and avoided as far as possible any mention of his own name. The ministry, pension and church extension funds were amongst those that benefited from his munificence. Likewise, the foreign mission work and the Church in Czechoslovakia.

Moravian churches in Northern Ireland and England, and the publication of books, also benefited from Sir John's generosity and that of the Purser family. Sir John and Professor Frederic Purser, Sir John's brother-in-law, helped to establish the Moravian Mission College at Bristol. Although he followed his mother's Moravian faith, Sir John gave £50 per year (1901-1938) to the Dublin Welsh Church or Bethel in Talbot Street (now a snooker hall), and also helped the Rev. John Lewis to purchase a house in Home Farm Road. Lewis was later to write a memoir of Purser Griffith's father, William Griffith. Purser Griffith never forgot his Welsh roots and purchased War Bonds, the interest on which went to the St. David's Society of Dublin.

Sir John was responsible in 1916 for funding a major extension to the Moravian church in Dublin. The Kevin Street extension was built by McLaughlin & Harvey, the architects being O'Callaghan & Webb. The work had been proposed as far back as 1900 and it was originally intended that John T.Purser would finance the project and that Purser Griffith would cover the cost of renovating the organ. As it turned out, Purser died in 1903 and Sir John's wife in 1912. Sir John initially agreed to contribute £5,000, but before building work could commence, costs escalated due to the "Rising", and he agreed to meet the increased cost in full. The church and extension, including some fine stained glass windows on the first floor assembly room, are still standing, although now used for different purposes, but always under threat of demolition.

Purser Griffith shared with Stoney a great love for and knowledge of both secular and church music. His knowledge of Moravian tunes and his interest in congregational singing found expression in the large contribution he made in 1911 to cover the cost of the musical edition of the Moravian Hymn Book. He, like his brother Frederick, and afterwards his son Frederick, played the organ at the church. His daughter Alice was an accomplished violinist and a patron of musicians. She was actively involved for many years in organising Feis Ceol and Royal Dublin Society concerts.

On the wider scene, Purser Griffith acted on the Financial Committee of the Moravian Church appointed at the Fulneck Synod of 1910. At the 1921 Synod he was unanimously appointed 'Secretarius Fratrum in Anglia', a senior lay position in the church, and in 1923, 'Advocatus Fratrum', or Brother Advocate.

Other benefactions

When he took over from Stoney at Dublin Port, Purser Griffith's salary as Engineer-in-Chief was only £933, rising to £1,000 by 1901. It is clear that his subsequent wealth was inherited through his wife from the Pursers. Following the death of his wife in 1912, Purser Griffith began to increase his financial support for a range of worthy causes and projects outside of the Moravian Church, in many cases anonymously, but probably in memory of his dear departed. Purser Griffith was thereafter to be cared for by his unmarried daughter Alice, who lived to the ripe old age of 89. He gave substantial sums of money to establish schemes in Trinity College Dublin for helping needy undergraduates and for making loans available to young graduates. Many hundreds of young doctors, engineers, clergymen and others were thereby helped in establishing themselves in their chosen careers.

Purser Griffith's niece, the celebrated portrait painter Sarah Purser, decided in 1934 that the main difficulty in filling directorship vacancies in the National Gallery was the lack of suitably qualified Irish candidates, and took action. In October, she commenced negotiations with TCD and University College Dublin, offering to endow an annual scholarship in the History of European Painting if both colleges would organise an examination for it in alternate years. She coaxed a sum equal to her proposed donation from Purser Griffith. The colleges agreed to her terms and UCD set up a course to prepare those who wished to take the examination. This project led eventually to the creation of degree courses, first at UCD and within a year at TCD, thus providing a cadre of Irish art historians. Thomas Bodkin, who was Honorary Professor of the History of Fine Arts at Trinity College Dublin, whilst in Dublin to examine candidates for the Purser Scholarship, wrote 'We all hope that the new opportunities which they have given the youth of Ireland will be accepted by many; and that a growing love and knowledge of the Fine Arts will spread from Trinity College to the nation at large.'

In 1931, the Royal Dublin Society celebrated its bicentenary, the President of the Society being the noted scientist, Professor John Joly. The Society decided to mark the occasion by awarding Purser Griffith, who had been elected to the position of Vice-President in 1922, its prestigious Boyle Medal. The presentation was made by Joly at a special bicentenary meeting of the society on 25th June of that year. Purser Griffith had supported a number of movements for research in Ireland. With his friend Dr Stevenson, Professor Joly had organised the Radium Institute in 1914. Lord Iveagh contributed £1,000, as did Sir John Purser Griffith a like amount, and the Society added a grant to the various smaller sums subscribed by its members. With this fund the Society purchased and preserved a supply of radium. The radium was kept intact, but the radon gas was pumped off, collected in phials, and issued for use to the medical profession. Further large sums of money were subscribed by Purser Griffith and others to purchase more radium. This activity ceased in 1952, when the Society handed over its stock of radium to the Cancer Association of Ireland.

Freedom of City of Dublin

The City Council decided to confer on Purser Griffith the Honorary Freedom of the City of Dublin 'in recognition of the pre-eminent position which he occupies in his profession, and in testimony of the esteem which he has earned by his long and distinguished record of service to the City and Port of Dublin and to the country generally.' 'With almost every scheme for developing our natural resources set on foot during the past forty years – whether it was concerned with electricity, the utilisation of peat, harbour construction or port improvements — the name of Sir John Purser Griffith has been associated.' 'The Poulaphuca Scheme will, when completed, remain a splendid monument, not only to their (Purser Griffith and Kettle) great engineering skill, but also to their untiring zeal for the public welfare.'

The presentation ceremony was held in a packed Council Chamber at City Hall on 8th June 1936, in the presence of his younger son, Frederick. The occasion was overshadowed to some extent by family events. Sir John's grandson, Evan, had been tragically killed the 'previous month in a motorcycle accident and his eldest son, John William had been diagnosed with throat cancer and was to die within two months.

In his speech, the Lord Mayor of Dublin, Alfie Byrne, said 'as now seems to be reasonably certain, we (are to) get supplies of electricity from the Bog of Allen as well as from Poulaphuca, let us not forget that our new Freeman was the really courageous pioneer in both fields of research and experiment. Of Sir John's good works in other than professional matters I can hardly dare to speak. All that I can safely say is that his advice and his means have been held at the disposal of civic and charitable efforts which are too numerous to recall. Regardless of political associations or of personal considerations he has contributed liberally to every kind of effort which he thought to be for the benefit of his fellow citizens. His name now adds new distinction to our distinguished and carefully guarded Roll of Honour, and it only remains for us to pray that he may long remain to guide us and to inspire us with high conceptions of civic duty.'

Grand old man of Irish engineering

Sir John Purser Griffith, one of the foremost members of the engineering profession in Ireland, died at his residence, Rathmines Castle, in the early hours of Friday, the 21st October, 1938, having been ill for only one week. A memorial service was held in London on the 23rd October and the funeral in Dublin the day following. Although the funeral was to be private, the Moravian Church was packed with mourners and sympathisers. The Minister, Brother Kunick, in a funeral address, said 'Sir John was a true Brother and friend, and a great Christian. His church attendance was exemplary and his life an inspiration. His outstanding characteristics were those of simplicity of heart and mind and soul, and mode of life, and a child-like faith, which made him so great that he could stand above all that was small.

Only a little more than two weeks earlier, on the occasion of his 90th birthday, an Irish Press reporter had asked Purser Griffith for his recipe of long life. 'I don't know that it is such a covetous thing', he had answered. 'I have been fortunate and have had good health.' He did admit, however, that he was a non-smoker. He had spent his birthday at a reunion with his family at "The Castle". Amongst the messages of congratulation was one from the President and Council of the Institution of Civil Engineers in London referring to his 'still active participation in engineering matters' an indication that he was indeed worthy of the description 'Grand Old Man of Irish Engineering.'

Only a little more than two weeks earlier, on the occasion of his 90th birthday, an Irish Press reporter had asked Purser Griffith for his recipe of long life. *'I don't know that it is such a covetous thing',* he had answered. *'I have been fortunate and have had good health.'* He did admit, however, that he was a non-smoker.

Rathmines Castle, Dublin

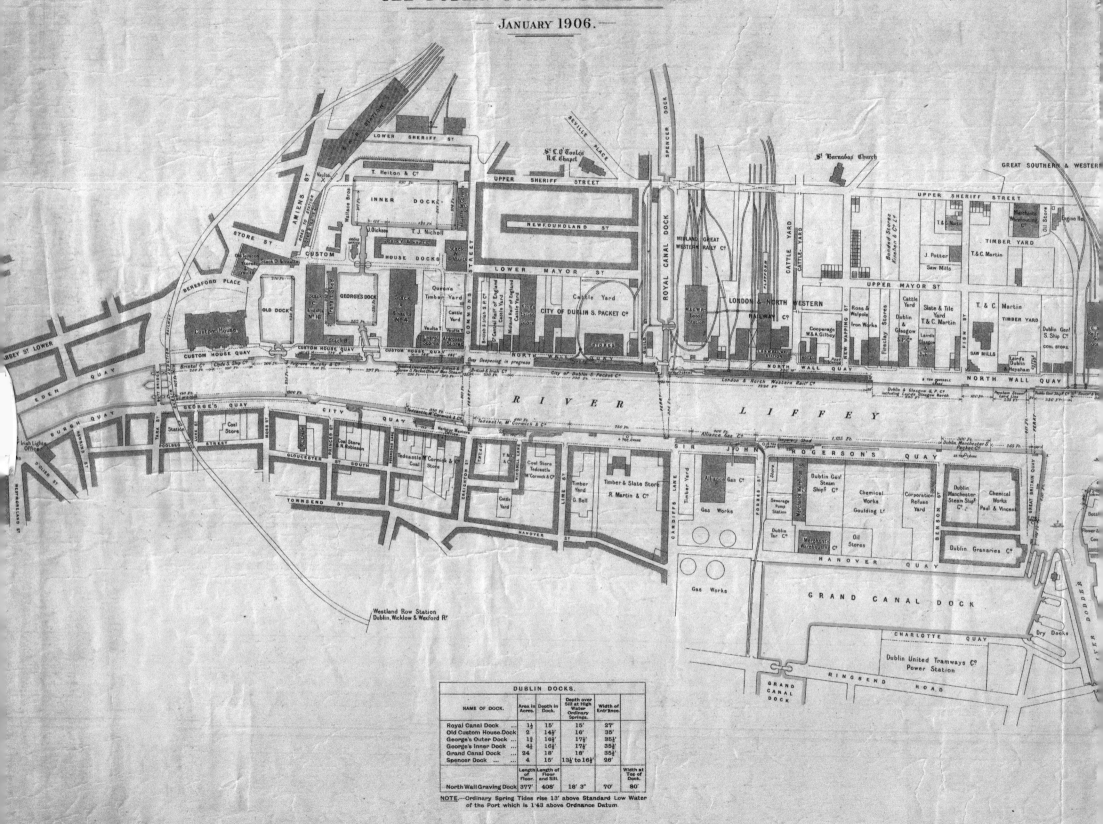

DUBLIN HARBOUR

PLAN OF SHIPPING QUAYS, SHEDS & TRAMWAY
under the jurisdiction of
THE DUBLIN PORT & DOCKS BOARD.

JANUARY 1906.

DUBLIN DOCKS.				
NAME OF DOCK.	Area in Acres.	Depth in Dock.	Depth over Sill at High Water Ordinary Springs.	Width of Entrance.
Royal Canal Dock ...	1½	15'	15'	27'
Old Custom House Dock	2	14½'	16'	35'
George's Outer Dock ...	1½	16½'	17½'	35½'
George's Inner Dock ...	4½	16½'	17½'	35½'
Grand Canal Dock ...	24	18'	18'	35½'
Spencer Dock ...	4	15'	13½' to 16½'	26'
	Length of Floor.	Length of Floor and Sill.		Width at Top of Dock.
North Wall Graving Dock	377'	408'	16' 3"	70'	80'

NOTE.— Ordinary Spring Tides rise 13' above Standard Low Water of the Port which is 1·43 above Ordnance Datum.